Bright & Beautiful

AUSTRALIAN
PATCHWORK
& QUILTING

Quilts

Craftworld Books

Contents

Tranquil Delights

The Power of Colour

Text Jan Stretton

Colour is a powerful tool which sets the mood of a quilt. It can be light and subtle, it can be dark and dramatic, it can be romantic and timeless or stylish and trendy. Just like a favourite song, colours conjure up happy associations from the past. It's strange that such an intrinsic part of our lives can be a cause for so much uncertainty when designing quilts.

When reading any text about colour and quilting, the same two words keep coming up - experience and confidence. Artists spend years playing with colour and confess to still learning in their old age. Monet devoted many of his later years to studying and painting the waterlily pond, never tiring of recreating the subtle nuances of colour to paint his large waterscape panels.

We all know too well how long it takes to make a quilt, so how can we achieve the necessary knowledge while we still have our faculties?

Working in other more immediate and less expensive media is one way. Study a colour wheel, or better still, colour your own. Get out the children's paints, crayons or coloured pencils and play around with them. You could also work with coloured paper, cutting up old magazines and used gift wrapping or buying pre-packaged craft sheets.

Quilters often baulk at using other media. Fabric is our chosen medium and that's what we want to work with! We love the added dimension which the texture of our materials brings to our work. We are compelled to get our hands on our fabric stash and usually don't want to spend time reading lengthy books about colour or taking extensive courses. Given these impatient desires, it is still possible to achieve the required experience and confidence.

When making quilts, the basic building blocks are colour, shape and pattern. Each element needs to work and harmonise with the other but it is the

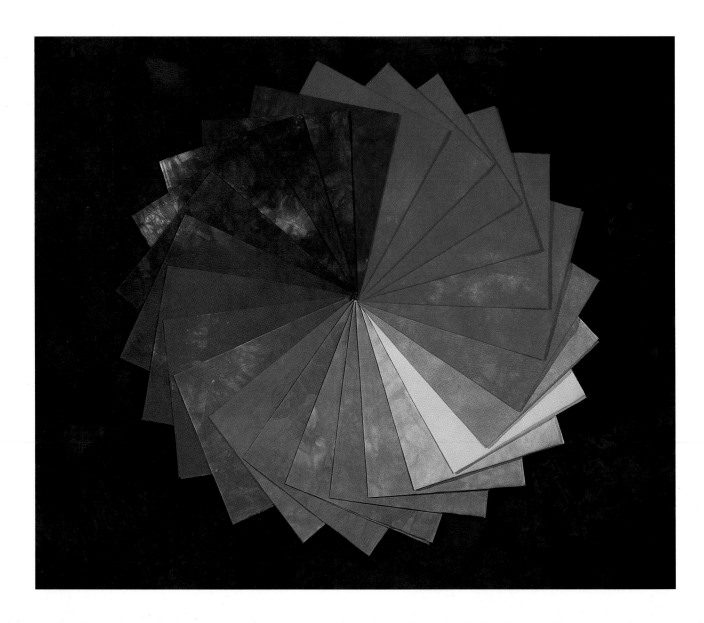

colour of a quilt which is the primary attraction. When showing a quilt, the first thing absorbed by the viewer is the colour.

Famous for his unfettered use of rich, glorious colour, English decorator Kaffe Fassett says, "Every one of us has the ability to create personal and warm-hearted decoration if we can only relax and let our confidence grow... so much detailed and finely coloured work has been done by uneducated hands. My own art training was less than a year."

With such encouragement, let's use our beloved fabrics and learn about colour. Firstly we need to recognise a flaw, one that is endemic to quilting and other craft workshops. Too often students enrol with the intention of taking something home. Always practical creatures, there is a need to have an end product to show for the time and money invested. Instead, look at the bigger picture. You are learning a technique you will find indispensable for the rest of your life – it doesn't have to be turned into a placemat or potholder to achieve relevance. Be content to see your work for what it is – a sample, to be referred to from time to time.

When making your experimental blocks, instead of stitching them, it is much simpler and quicker to use heavy card as backing and glue-stick the pieces into place. Ensure that you don't leave any gaps between the pieces, as this can detract from the overall effect. Choose a block which is not too complicated, but has a sufficient number of pieces to enable playing around. Card Trick is a good one to experiment with, as it shows graphically how much the look of the block is changed by the colour choices and placement.

Before you cut into your fabrics, select about a dozen different squares from your collection (or visit a fabric shop and use the bolts). Take a few steps back and look at them through half-squinted eyes. Does one colour stand out? Is there a range of light to dark or do the colours seem to merge together?

As you cut your pieces of fabric and start laying out your blocks, ask yourself some questions. What happens when strong lights are placed beside strong and darks? Do colours affect mood? What happens when you use just one colour and change the intensity? What happens to a colour when you change the surrounding colours? If you use only prints or only solids, what effect does it have on the look of the block? If you use only pale shades do you lose the dramatic effect of the block design?

To help find the answers, let's get back to basics.

BASICS OF COLOUR

❖

Hue The three primary colours are red, blue and yellow and, because no other colours can be mixed together to produce them, they provide the strongest contrasts. If you arrange them in a circle, you can create the secondary colours by mixing each of two adjacent primaries. The secondaries, violet, orange and green, are less intense because they are mixtures. You can continue on, mixing adjacent colours to achieve more gradations of colour.

Making a fabric colour wheel is an eye-opening exercise which can highlight the weaknesses in your collection. It is not uncommon for favourite colours to predominate, but often there may be shelves of blue, and no orange or yellow. It is a good opportunity to rectify this oversight and add a previously 'forbidden' hue to your stocks. As American quilter and colour doyenne, Mary Coyne Penders, says, "You can't cook with colour if the cupboard is bare!"

EXERCISE: Make a colour wheel of primary and secondary colours.

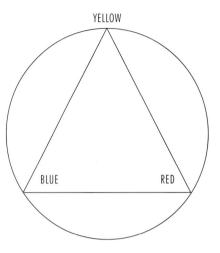

Primary Colours

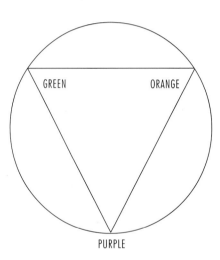

Secondary Colours

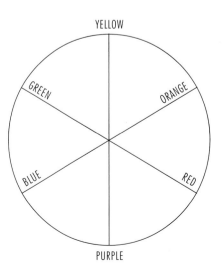

Complementary or Opposite Colours

Complementary Colours When you combine a coordinated range of fabric in a quilt top, the result is often unsatisfactory. Your eye is looking for harmony which is achieved when the colours balance each other. This happens when colours from opposite sides of the colour wheel are juxtaposed. These opposing colours are called complementary and their successful use is a prerequisite for good quilt design.

To gain an understanding of colour and how it works, study art and quilt books and magazines. Choose paintings or quilts that particularly appeal to you and then refer to their placement on the colour wheel. In this way, you will accumulate a working knowledge of how your preferred colour combinations relate to each other and why you find them pleasing.

The paintings of Matisse are so successful because his compositions are a continuous adjustment of colour to colour, shape to shape and colour to shape. Matisse had a gift for finding new and unusual colour combinations as well as exploiting old favourites. His painting Red Room (Harmony in Red) features the traditional colours of Christmas, red and green, which are opposite each other on the colour wheel. The painting, a contrast of warm and cool colours with straight and curved lines, creates a feeling of balance and serenity, also evident in quilts made in such colour combinations.

EXERCISE: Take colours that are opposite each other on the colour wheel and use them to make a block of your own choosing. As you construct the block, observe how one colour changes the appearance of the other. You can repeat this exercise with a different combination of colours.

Value A colour's value is the result of mixing a pure hue with black (creating a shade), or white (creating a tint) or with grey (resulting in a tone). Fabric design relies heavily on contrasting values and the application of changing values is integral to the way a block presents in a quilt. Many very successful quilts are made in one colour, but with different values of that colour.

EXERCISE: Make a block (eg Card Trick) using only one colour in a range of values. The greater the difference in value, the more dramatic the effect. Make the same block again, but this time change the position of the different values and observe the changed design.

Card Trick Block

Working with the same hue can be visually tedious and often requires a small addition of another colour for relief.

SATURATION OR INTENSITY

Colour is considered pure and most intense when it has not been diluted with any complementary colour, or black and white. Many quilters shy away from such strength in their colour, while others splash it about with gay abandon. Wonderful, vibrant creations can be made from all pure colours, while other quilters achieve their dramatic effect by just a suggestion of saturated colour.

Study the quilts made by the Amish, who have a special gift for turning simple, pieced designs into bold adventures with colour.

EXERCISE: Make a block such as Log Cabin, using your brightest, purest colours. It is preferable to use a simple block for this exercise, to let the colours 'do the talking'. You may need to refer to your colour wheel to check on the colour saturation.

Traditional Log Cabin Block

Miniature Log Cabin Blocks

WARM OR COOL

Each colour has a 'temperature', the extremes being red-orange, which is the warmest, and blue-green, which is the coolest. Colour temperature has a powerful influence on your quilt designs. Colour temperature is relative and its effect depends on its surroundings. If you place a colour in the medium range next to red-orange, it will seem cool. When placed next to blue-green, it will appear warm.

EXERCISE: Make a striped block, placing cool colours next to warm.

Having made your block, pin it on the wall and observe how the warm colours advance, while the cool ones seem to recede. Colour is the builder of the space and your choice of colours will dictate the impact. If you choose a pure red as your main colour, it will command attention from all other colours around it. When yellow is placed next to a deep colour, such as purple, it appears strong, yet it fades beside a pale pastel!

THE DRAMA OF BLACK AND WHITE

❖

Has your quiltmaking been a little timid? Have you been avoiding using black? Even when small amounts of black are incorporated in a quilt, it can intensify the other colours. Again, we turn to the Amish for inspiration. They have not allowed their sombre outdoor clothing to turn them off using black in their quilts. The creative freedom so evident in their quilts often involves the use of exuberant, bright colours next to black. Amish women recognised inherently the pleasing combinations of colours. Their approach is fresh and open, as they are not swayed by the current marketplace and the dictates of changing fashions in home decorating.

We have learnt that complemetary colours give contrast to a quilt, but we can also add intensity and depth by incorporating black and white. Placing black and white side by side creates a dramatic contrast which decreases as the black is lightened through various shades of grey.

EXERCISE: Choose a block, such as Jacob's Ladder or Storm at Sea, and make it three times, using prints or solids. In the first sample, restrict yourself to using black, white or grey. Repeat the block, this time combining colours with black. Make a third block, substituting the black with white. Pin your three blocks up and study the differences in each.

EXPERIENCE AND CONFIDENCE

❖

As you make your blocks and become more confident with your own choices, you realise that working with colour is not an intellectual exercise, but a feeling. You relate personally to the colours and develop a natural affinity for certain colour relationships. It's all about following your own path, making quilts which reflect your own tastes and style, and feeling pride in your work. ✳

Storm at Sea Block in strong, bright colours.

Storm at Sea Block in pastel colours.

Below: Cushion made with a Jacob's Ladder Block in bright colours.

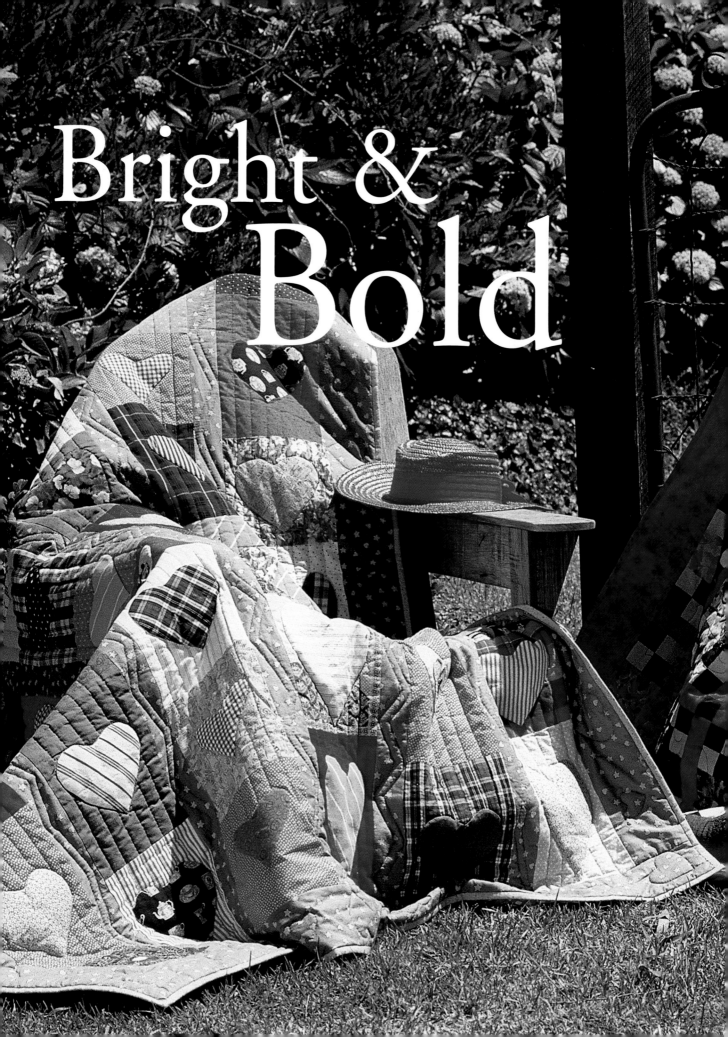

Bright &
Bold

Beatte's Heart Scrap Quilt

When requested by her daughter to make a heart quilt as a throwover using freehand drawn hearts and base colours of purple and orange, Penny Lanser decided to appliqué hearts onto random block sizes using existing fabrics in her stash. After that the quilt just happened, with Penny working out the final arrangement once the blocks were completed.

PREPARATION

❖

Decide upon the size and shape of your hearts. Penny made three sizes – small, medium and large. Draw the heart shapes onto cardboard and cut out to use as templates.

CUTTING

❖

When cutting the hearts leave an extra 6mm (¼in) seam allowance.

From your assorted scrap fabrics cut,
– 13 large hearts
– 29 medium hearts
– 19 small hearts.

For each heart, cut a piece of fusible webbing exactly the same size as the template and laid on the reverse side.

Also from your assorted scrap fabrics cut 61 blocks, 19.5cm (7⅝in) in width and varying in length from 15cm to 28cm (6in to 11in).

From the length of your choice of border/sashing fabric, cut:
– four, 10cm (4½in) lengths for the borders
– five, 6cm (2½in) lengths for the sashing strips.

From the width of the binding fabric, cut:
– eight, 4cm (1⅝in) strips.

ASSEMBLY

❖

Turn under and baste the raw edges of each heart 6mm (¼in) all around, easing at the V and at the corners to keep the edge as smooth as possible.

Iron a fusible-webbing heart onto the wrong side of each heart and then iron the heart in the centre of a rectangular block. Remove the basting stitches and blind-sew the edges of the heart to the block.

When all the blocks are completed, arrange them in strips to suit yourself, trying to balance the colours and sizes. Sew the blocks together into six strips, making sure that the strips end up the same length. It may be necessary to adjust the block lengths to ensure this happens.

When Penny had assembled her strips of hearts she decided to add another small heart-shape cut out with pinking shears and embroidered to the heart block with black embroidery thread and running stitches to some heart blocks.

A button was sewn into the centre of these and onto other randomly selected blocks.

Starting at the outside with a 10cm border strip, sew on a strip of hearts, then a 6cm sashing strip, a strip of hearts, another 6cm sashing strip and continue across the quilt ending with another 10cm border strip. Finish the quilt top by sewing a 10cm border strips on the top and bottom edges.

BACKING

❖

After choosing her backing fabric, Penny found there was only enough in the shop to just manage, meaning she would have to cut it carefully to make it fit. As a result, she ended up with a patch in one corner. Consequently, she added three small blocks of contrast colours to complete the backing. If you have any leftover hearts, you could do the same. However from the given yardage, remove the selvedge, cut in half and join horizontally.

Cut and piece backing fabric so that it is 2in larger on all sides than the quilt top. Layer the backing fabric, batting and quilt top and baste the three layers together.

FINISHED QUILT SIZE

- 155cm x 245cm (61in x 96.5in)

MATERIALS

- 4.5m (4⅞yd) total of scrap fabrics in desired colours (Penny used 32 different fabrics)
- 3.2m (3½yd) backing fabric
- 2.3m (2½yd) border/sashing fabric
- 45cm (½yd) binding fabric
- 170cm x 260cm (67in x 102in) batting
- 1m (1⅛yd) fusible webbing
- Scraps of cardboard
- Pencil and paper
- Erasable fabric pen
- 1cm (⅜in) and 2.5cm (1in) wide masking tape
- Matching sewing thread
- Quilting cotton
- Black embroidery thread
- Unusual buttons
- General sewing supplies
- Pinking shears

NOTE: Requirements are based on 100 per cent cotton, prewashed and ironed 112cm (44in) wide fabric.

Above left: Turn raw edges under ⅛in and baste around each heart. Iron a same sized, fusible-webbing heart onto the wrong side.

Below left: Iron the heart into the centre of a rectangular block and then remove the basting stitches.

Above right: Using thread to match the appliquéd piece, blind-sew the edges of the heart to the block.

QUILTING

Hand or machine-quilt your quilt as desired. Penny quilted around the hearts first then, using the 2.5cm (1in) masking tape as a guide, quilted vertical stripes up to the hearts, but not through them. In the sashings, she used the 1cm (³/₈in) masking tape to make a zigzag pattern. The border was quilted in alternate medium and small heart shapes.

BINDING

Join the binding strips together and press in half lengthwise, wrong sides together. Stitch to the sides of the quilt first and fold over to the back of the quilt and slip-stitch in place. Then attach the binding to the top and bottom of the quilt, folding in the ends of the binding strips to neaten them. ✳

Spring Fever

Black and white Four Patch blocks add a dramatic effect to this gorgeous quilt designed and made by Ann Langley. A perfect way to display an array of favourite colourful prints, all accented by dramatic red sashings and border fabrics.

CUTTING

From the black homespun, cut 20, 2in strips across the fabric.

From the cream homespun, cut 20, 2in strips across the fabric.

From each of the print fabrics cut the following number and sizes of squares:

Fabric	No of 3⅞in squares	No of 3½in squares
Yellow	6	24
Orange	4	16
Light red	6	24
Dark red	4	16
Violet	6	24
Light blue-green	6	24
Dark blue-green	6	24
Light yellow-green	6	24
Dark yellow-green	4	16

From the red sashing fabric cut 82, 2in x 9½in rectangles.

From the black homespun, cut 35, 2in squares and four, 4½in corner squares.

From the red border fabric, cut seven, 4½in strips across the fabric.

Also from the red border fabric, cut eight, 2¼in strips for the binding.

CONSTRUCTION

Each block has four black and cream four-patch squares, one half-square triangle patch made from two of the print fabrics and two squares of each of the prints used in the half-square triangle patch as shown in the Block Diagram.

Sew one black 2in homespun strip to a cream 2in homespun strip and press the seam towards the black. Crosscut the strip at right angles to the seam into 2in segments. Sew the segments together, reversing the position of the squares to achieve a Four Patch. Press the seam open. Make a total of 192 of these patches. See diagram 1.

Prepare the centre triangle squares using the 3⅞in squares cut from the print fabrics. Combine the squares in the following combinations to make the number of triangle squares specified:

4 x light red/orange
8 x yellow/dark yellow-green
12 x light yellow-green/dark blue-green
12 x light blue green/violet
8 x light red/dark red
4 x yellow/orange

To make the first triangle square, take a light red, 3⅞in square and a orange 3⅞in

Diagram 1

Diagram 2

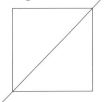
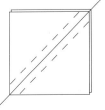

Block Diagram

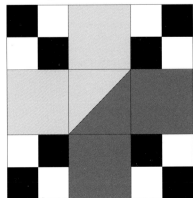

Above: Combine the 3⅞in print fabric squares to make the triangle squares.

Below: Sew the black and cream strips together, crosscut into 2in segments and then sew the segments together to create four-patch units.

square, placing them right sides together. Mark a diagonal line on the wrong side of the lighter fabric. Machine ¼in on each side of the drawn line and cut apart on the drawn line to yield two red/orange triangle squares. Press the seam to the darker fabric. Repeat once more with this combination to obtain the required four triangle squares.

Use the same procedure to make the remaining 44 triangle squares required.

ASSEMBLY

Lay out each block, selecting the 3½in squares to correspond with the triangle square in the middle.

Join the squares to make rows, then join the rows to make the block. Prepare all 48 blocks.

NOTE: Take care to arrange the black patches correctly as it is easy to make a mistake here!

SASHING

Lay out the blocks with reference to the quilt colour photo on page 18. Take care that the triangle squares are arranged correctly.

Sew a 2in x 9½in red sashing rectangle between the blocks as you join them into rows. Press the seams towards the sashings.

Sew a 2in x 9½in red sashing rectangle between the 2in black homespun squares to make the horizontal sashing strips. Press the seams to the sashings.

Join the rows together to make the quilt centre, press the seams to the sashings.

The quilt top should now measure 62in x 83in.

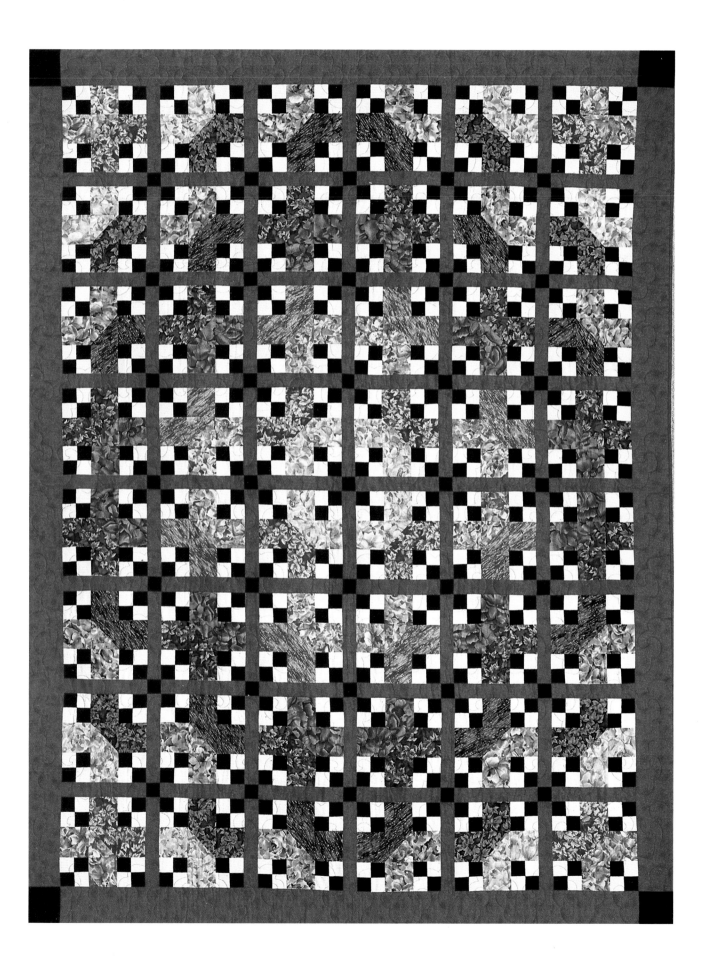

BORDER

Join the 4½in border strips to give two, 83in vertical borders and two, 62in horizontal borders.

Sew the vertical borders to each side of the quilt and carefully press the seams to the borders.

Sew a black corner square to both ends of the horizontal borders and press the seams to the borders. Sew the border strips to the top and bottom of the quilt. Press the seams to the borders.

The pieced quilt top should now measure 70in x 91in.

QUILTING

Cut the backing fabric into two, 2.5m (98½in) lengths and sew together along one side. Trim the selvedges along the seam and press the seam open.

Layer the backing fabric, wadding and quilt top and pin or baste as usual.

Complete the quilting as desired. Ann had her quilt machine quilted by Bronwyn Lane of Bronnie's Machine Quilting Service in an all-over fleur-de-lis design using red thread. Trim the edges of the quilt when the quilting is completed.

BINDING

Join the 2¼in binding strips and, with wrong sides together, press in half along the length. Sew to the top of the quilt, aligning all raw edges and mitring the corners as you go.

Turn the folded edges over to the back of the quilt's and hand-sew in place.

Add a label on the back to document your quilt particulars.   ✳

Above: Lay out the units for each block selecting 3½in squares to correspond with the triangle square in the middle.

Below: A completed block.

Citrus

A vibrant array of citrus colours is combined in this delightful miniature quilt by Kerry Gadd, who includes her tips for accurate piecing which is so important when working with such tiny pieces of fabric.

FINISHED BLOCK SIZE

• 8cm (3in)

FINISHED QUILT SIZE

• 46cm x 54.5cm (18in x 21½in)

MATERIALS

• 40cm (½yd) green print fabric

• 20cm (¼yd) lime green fabric

• 10cm (⅛yd) bright yellow fabric

• 20cm (¼yd) background fabric

• 10cm (⅛yd) black and white print for sashings

• 56cm x 65cm (22in x 25½in) piece of backing fabric

• 56cm x 65cm (22in x 25½in) Pellon

• Sewing thread: neutral for piecing, green for outer border and thread for machine quilting

• Rotary cutter, mat and rulers

• Bias square ruler (this is essential)

• Scissors, long quilters pins, quick unpick, tape measure, sewing machine and accessories

NOTE: This small quilt is based on the Variable Star block. It is made up of 12, 3in blocks, set 3 x 4, separated by ½in-wide sashing strips.

Press all seams open unless otherwise instructed. Fabric requirements are based on 112cm (44in) wide fabric.

SEAM ALLOWANCE TEST

Accuracy in cutting and sewing is very important during construction.
All cutting instructions include ¼in seam allowance. An accurate ¼in seam allowance must be sewn throughout the construction process. If you are not sure do this simple test. Cut three strips of fabric 1½in x 3in. Sew them together along the long edges to form a strip unit. Press the seams open. The width of the centre strip must measure 1in.

Refer to Diagram 1.

CUTTING

From the green print fabric, cut:
– two, 4in strips for the borders
– two, 2¼in strips across the fabric width.

With the two narrower strips layered together, cut 24, 2¼in squares. Cut these squares diagonally once to yield 24 half-square triangles.

From the bright yellow fabric, cut:
– one, 2¼in strip across the fabric width.

Cut this into 12, 2¼in squares. Cut these diagonally once to yield 24 half-square triangles.

From the lime green fabric, cut:
– two, 1⅜in strips across the fabric width for binding
– one, 1½in strip across the fabric width.

From this strip cut 12, 1½in squares for block centres and six, 1in squares for the sashing posts.

From the background fabric, cut:
– one, 2¼in strip across the fabric width.

Cut this strip into 12, 2¼in squares and cut these once diagonally to yield 24 half-square triangles.

– two, 1½in strips across the fabric width

Cut this strip into 48, 1½in squares. From the black and white print fabric, cut:
– three, 1in strips across the fabric width for sashing strips. These will be cut to size later.

CONSTRUCTION

To each of the 24 yellow triangles sew 24 of the green print triangles. Sew the remaining 24 green triangles to the 24 background fabric triangles. Press the

seams open. The resulting bias squares must measure 1⅞in.

Cut all 48 of these bias squares in half diagonally.

TIP

Cut carefully as the top corner of the bias square will try to move as you come to it. To avoid this, after lining up the bias-square ruler diagonally through the corners, press the rotary cutter blade firmly onto the seam to pre-cut through some of the seam allowance bulk. Now cut normally.

You will end up with two sets of triangles from each fabric combination, each a mirror image of its mate. As you cut, keep them in separate piles according to their fabric placement.

Sew a green/yellow triangle unit to a green/background triangle unit. Be gentle, as you will be sewing on bias edges. Press the seam open. The resulting square will measure exactly 1½in. Repeat with all the remaining triangle units.

Lay out the pieces for a block as shown in the Block Assembly Diagram. Follow the piecing diagram and construct one block. Press the seams in the direction of the arrows. The resulting block will measure 3½in. Make 11 more blocks. It is always a good idea to make one block first to make sure it is correct. Then proceed to chain-piece the remaining blocks together.

ASSEMBLY

From the pre-cut black and white sashing fabric, cut 17 short strips 3½in x 1in. Lay out the blocks beside your machine, in four rows of three blocks each. Leave a gap between them.

Place a sashing strip to the right-hand side of the first block in each row and sew in place. Join the blocks together to form four rows of three blocks. Press the seams towards the sashing strips.

Use the remaining nine sashing strips and the six lime green 1in squares to make three long horizontal sashing strips as shown in the Sashing Strip Diagram. Press seams in the direction of the arrows shown on the Block Assembly Diagram.

Sew a long sashing strip to the bottom of the first three blocks. Continue joining the rows together with sashing strips between to form the quilt top. Press the seams towards the sashing strips.

Measure the quilt horizontally through the centre from edge to edge. Cut two strips of sashing fabric this length. Fold each strip in half to find the centre and mark it with a pin. Do the same for the top and bottom edges of the quilt. Sew the strips in place, matching the pins. Press towards the sashing.

For the sides of the quilt, measure vertically through the centre from edge to edge and repeat as above.

BORDERS

❖

Measure the quilt horizontally through the centre from edge to edge. Cut two strips this measurement, cutting one strip from each of the 4in-wide border strips. Pin mark the centre of both strips and the top and bottom edges of the quilt. Match the pins and sew in place to the sides of the quilt. Press the seams towards the borders.

Measure the quilt vertically through the centre from edge to edge. Mark this measurement onto the two remaining strips. Pin mark the centre on the strips and the sides, then sew to edges of quilt. Press the seams towards the borders.

Diagram 1 – Seam allowance test

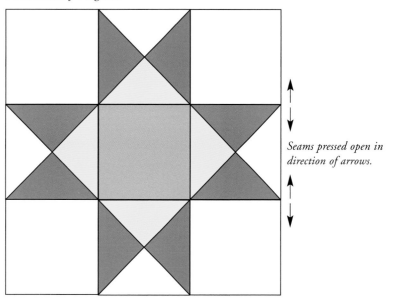

Piecing Diagrams.

Press seams in direction of arrows.

Block Assembly Diagram.

Seams pressed open in direction of arrows.

Sashing Strip Diagram.

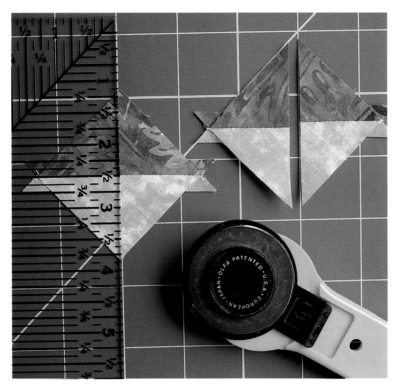

Above: Line up the bias-square ruler diagonally through the corners and press the rotary cutter blade onto the seam to pre-cut through the seam allowance before cutting through the square.

Below: Sew a green/yellow triangle unit to a green/background triangle unit. The resulting square should measure 1½in. Lay out the pieces for each block and join them to form a 3½in block.

QUILTING

Place the backing fabric, right side down, onto a firm surface. Lightly tape the corners in position to hold in place.

Place the batting over this and tape in place. Finally lay the pressed quilt top over the batting. Tape this in place as well.

Pin baste in the centre of all the blocks then around the outside seam line of the outer sashing strips, just into the outer border. Remove the tape.

Machine quilt in the ditch around each block, then in the outer sashing strip seam next to the outer border, removing the pins as you get to them.

Lay the quilt back onto the flat surface and pin baste all around the outer edges of the borders.

Machine quilt a design of your choice in the border. This can be free motion or a stencilled design.

After quilting, use the rotary cutter to neaten the edges of the quilt, trimming the outer border to 3½in wide.

BINDING

Cut the two, 1⅜in strips in half to yield four strips. These are measured and attached in the same manner as for the outer borders.

Sew the bindings to the quilt using a ¼in seam allowance resulting in a ¼in-wide binding. The turn under of the seam allowance at the back is generous. When attaching the side bindings, leave enough fabric extending at both ends to turn over and cover the raw edges.

Sign and date your quilt on the back. ✳

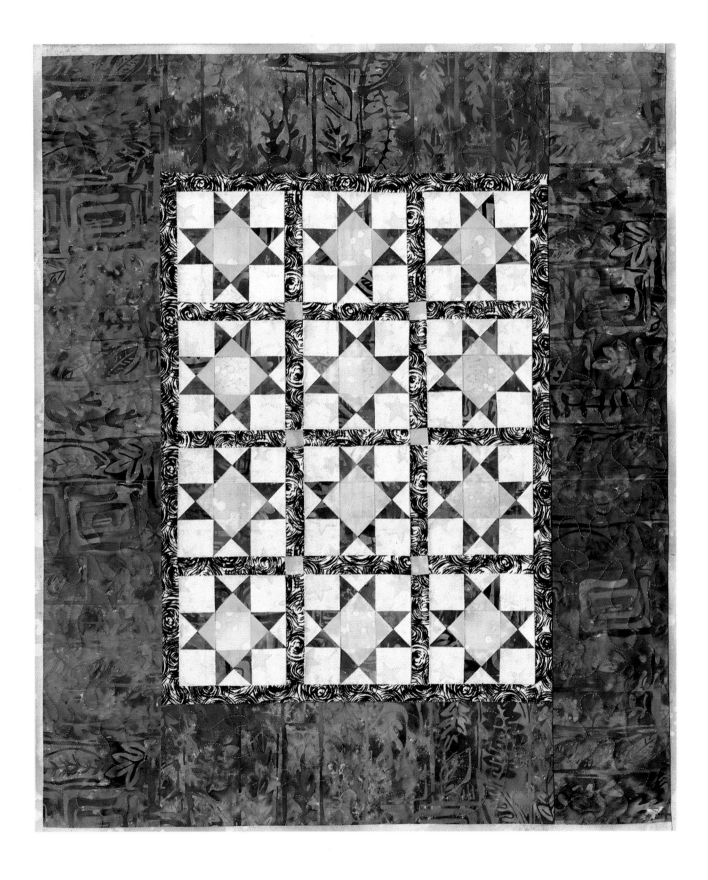

Acapulco

Inspired by tales of her daughter's working holiday in Mexico and the wonderful array of colours available in hand-dyed fabrics, Caroline Price designed this inspirational wall-hanging using double-sided fusible webbing, satin stitch and machine quilting.

PREPARATION

Remove the selvedges from the background fabric. The quilt is made with the edges of the background fabric at the top and bottom of the quilt. Trace the full quilt pattern from the pattern sheet onto a large piece of paper. Lay a piece of dressmaker's carbon paper, carbon-side down, onto the background fabric. Place the traced appliqué on top, and draw around each shape, just inside the design lines, with a ballpoint pen. It is not necessary to draw the full shape but just enough to give an accurate guide for placement of the appliqué pieces. By tracing just inside the design lines, the appliqué pieces will cover any drawn lines.

APPLIQUE

Trace a mirror image of each of the appliqué pieces, tracing from the wrong side of the pattern directly onto the paper backing of the fusible webbing. Remember to add a seam allowance to any edge which will be placed under another appliqué piece. Cut out each of the shapes, leaving approximately ¼in around each piece. Iron the fusible webbing to the wrong side of the selected fabric.

Cut out the appliqué shapes carefully on the pencil line and peel away the paper lining. The pieces are then positioned and ironed into place on the quilt top. Note that the leaves are ironed and sewn first, using the numbers on each leaf shown on the pattern sheet as both an ironing and sewing guide. The flowers and birds are ironed and stitched on last.

SATIN STITCHING

Satin stitch is a close zigzag stitch with a very short stitch length.

Before satin stitching around the appliqué pieces, place a piece of tear-away stabiliser behind the work to help prevent the appliqué shape from puckering.

When you satin stitch it may be necessary to reduce the top tension on your machine to prevent the bobbin thread from pulling to the top.

Caroline uses a Bernina sewing machine which has a finger on the bobbin case through which the bobbin thread can be threaded. If you are using a Bernina machine, follow this step and it may not be necessary to reduce the top tension.

Sew the satin stitching so that the majority of the stitch is on the appliqué piece and just a little bit is on the background fabric. Always try to commence stitching on a straight line of the appliqué piece.

To prevent having to lock off the threads or pull them through to the back, stitch a tiny straight stitch for about ¼in which will later be covered by the satin stitch, and trim the thread tails.

It is recommended to prepare several practice appliqué shapes and experiment to make sure your machine settings and tension are correct.

The secret to sewing even curves when satin stitching is to pivot with the needle down on the width of the curve. On tight curves, you may have to lower the needle and pivot the work every few stitches.

Using an open-toed appliqué foot, satin-stitch all the appliqué pieces using a stitch width of approximately 1.5-2mm. The stitch length is the same as for the buttonholes.

FINISHED QUILT SIZE

70cm x 90cm (27½in x 35in)

MATERIALS

- 15cm x 25cm (6in x 10in) of both light and dark orange fabrics for Bird 1
- 20cm x 25cm (8in x 10in) aqua fabric for Bird 2
- 10cm x 25cm (4in x 10in) bright yellow fabric for Bird 2
- 15cm x 25cm (6in x 10in) cyclamen fabric for Bird 3
- 10cm x 25cm (4in x 10in) purple fabric for Bird 3
- 10cm (4in) square of dark yellow fabric for Bird 3
- 15cm x 25cm (6in x 10in) green fabric for Bird 4
- 10cm x 25cm (4in x 10in) russet fabric for Bird 4
- Scraps of red, jade green, marigold, yellow, orange, cyclamen, violet, gold, aqua and violet are used for the flowers A, B, C, D and E
- Scraps of a large variety of different coloured fabrics up to 30cm (12in) long are required for the leaves
- 80cm (⅞yd) blue background fabric
- 1.1m (1¼yd) fabric for backing and rod pocket
- 30cm (⅓yd) binding fabric
- 90cm x 100cm (35½in x 40in) batting
- 1.5m x 30cm (1⅝yd x 12in) double-sided fusible webbing
- 1.2m x 50cm (1⅜yd x 20in) tear-away fabric stabiliser
- Rayon machine embroidery threads to match fabrics
- Bobbinfil or lightweight thread for bobbin
- Monofilament thread for quilting
- Dark blue rayon machine embroidery thread for quilting
- Regular sewing thread for attaching binding
- Dressmaker's carbon paper and ballpoint pen
- Large sheet of paper to trace full-sized pattern
- Scissors, both paper and fabric
- Open-toed appliqué foot
- Rotary cutter, ruler and mat
- Sewing machine and general sewing supplies

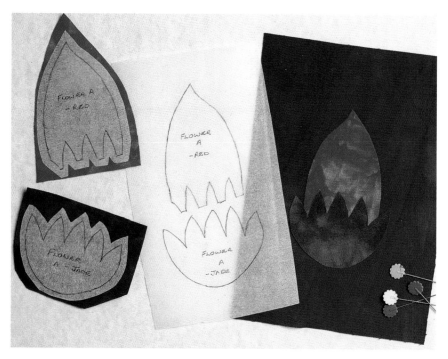

Above: Trace the appliqué shapes onto the paper backing of the fusible webbing. Iron the webbing to the wrong side of your chosen fabric, cut out carefully on the pencil line and iron into position.

QUILTING

From one selvedge edge of the backing fabric, cut a strip 6½in x 27in and put this aside for the rod pocket.

Press the appliquéd top carefully. Layer the backing fabric, batting and quilt top and baste the three layers together. Caroline machine-quilted around each of the appliqué shapes using monofilament thread on the top of the machine and regular sewing thread to match the backing fabric in the bobbin. The background was then stipple-quilted using a matching coloured, rayon embroidery thread in the top of the machine. Both types of machine quilting were done using the free-motion method, that is, with a quilting or darning foot and the feed dogs lowered.

Because both the appliqué and stipple quilting can distort a quilt top, it is necessary to square up the top before the binding is sewn on. A large, builder's set square is ideal for this task but two large rulers can be used to ensure that the top is perfectly squared. Trim the quilt top to 35in x 27½in.

BINDING

From the width of the binding fabric, cut four, 2¼in strips. Stitch the strips into one long length with 45-degree seams. Press the seams open. Press the length of the binding in half, wrong sides together. Using a ¼in seam, stitch the binding around the edge of the quilt top, with all raw edges even and mitring at each corner.

Hem each of the short ends of the 6½in x 27in rod pocket strip. Fold the strip in half lengthwise, wrong sides together. Pin the folded rod pocket to the back of the quilt with the raw edges even with the quilt. Stitch the rod pocket in place, sewing just above the previous line of the binding stitches.

Fold the binding to the back of the quilt and firmly hand-stitch in place. Move up the folded edge of the rod pocket approximately ¼in, creating a slight bulge of fabric at the top of the rod pocket. Pin and hand stitch the folded edge securely to the quilt back. The hanging rod will sit into this bulge, so that when you position your quilt on the wall it will sit flat rather than buckling.

Don't forget to sign and date your beautiful, new wall-hanging. ✳

> ### NOTE
>
> Caroline used 22 different coloured rayon machine-embroidery threads in her quilt. If you do not have a large selection of machine-embroidery threads, try an old gold colour which seems to go with most fabrics. It is recommended that the fabric be 100 per cent cotton, pre-washed and ironed. Requirements for the background, backing and binding fabrics are based on 112cm (44in) wide fabric.

Antique Log Cabin

*Strong, eye-catching colours are often found in antique quilts such
as this Barn Raising Log Cabin from Narelle Grieve's collection. So that you
can make your own version of this delightful old quilt, we asked
Wendy Wilson to write up the instructions.*

CUTTING

NOTE: All fabric requirements are based on 110cm (42in) wide fabric. It is recommended all fabrics be 100 per cent cotton. Pre-wash and iron your fabrics before beginning to cut.

All cutting instructions are for cutting across the width of the fabric. A $\frac{1}{4}$in seam allowance has been included in all cutting requirements.

From the mid blue fabric, cut:
– 36, 3in squares.

From the dark green small print fabrics, cut:
– 36, $1\frac{1}{2}$in x 3in
– 36, $1\frac{1}{2}$in x 4in
– 36, $1\frac{1}{2}$in x 7in
– 36, $1\frac{1}{2}$in x 8in.

From the yellow small print fabrics, cut:
– 36, $1\frac{1}{2}$in x 4in
– 36, $1\frac{1}{2}$in x 5in
– 36, $1\frac{1}{2}$in x 8in
– 36, $1\frac{1}{2}$in x 9in.

From the dark red with dark spot fabric, cut:
– 36, $1\frac{1}{2}$in x 5in
– 36, $1\frac{1}{2}$in x 6in
– 36, $1\frac{1}{2}$in x 9in
– 36, $1\frac{1}{2}$in x 10in.

From the pink small print fabrics, cut:
– 36, $1\frac{1}{2}$in x 6in
– 36, $1\frac{1}{2}$in x 7in
– 36, $1\frac{1}{2}$in x 10in
– 36, $1\frac{1}{2}$in x 11in.

From the rust red first border fabric, cut:
– six, 3in strips.

From the pink outer border fabric, cut down the length of the fabric:
– three, 7in strips.

BLOCK CONSTRUCTION

Place all the strips in order as shown in the photo on page 31. This will assist in the order of placement.

With right sides together, sew a shorter green log to one side of each mid blue centre square with a $\frac{1}{4}$in seam allowance. To save time, feed one unit directly behind the next through your sewing machine. Continue in this manner until all 36 blocks are done. This method also saves thread. It is important that the top and bottom edges of the fabric pieces line up perfectly. Use pins to prevent slipping.

Clip the threads between the units and press the seam away from the centre. Then place the units in a stack, right sides facing up and green strip at the bottom.

With right sides together, place the second green log to the right of the square keeping the first log at the bottom of each unit. Feed through the machine as before. Clip threads, press and place units in a stack with the last green log at the bottom.

Place the first yellow strip to the new right side of the centre square (was originally the top), coming over the last green log. Machine-piece in the same way as before, taking care to keep the top and bottom edges together. Cut threads and press away from the centre square. Place in a stack with the last log on the bottom. Add the second yellow log, machine piecing as before. Cut threads and press.

Continue in the same way adding the logs in the order you laid them out and rotating the units clockwise each time so that the last log is placed at the bottom of the stack before the next log is added.

After the yellow come two red, two pink, two green, two yellow, two reds, finishing with two pinks. These are the last logs in the block. Remember to keep pressing between each addition of logs. It is important that the top and bottom

FINISHED BLOCK SIZE
• 26.5cm (10$\frac{1}{2}$in)

FINISHED QUILT SIZE
• 203cm x 181.5cm (80in x 71$\frac{1}{2}$in)

MATERIALS
• 30cm ($\frac{1}{3}$yd) mid blue fabric for centre squares
• 50cm ($\frac{1}{2}$yd) dark green small print fabrics
• 1.3m (1$\frac{3}{8}$yd) dark red with dark spot fabric
• 1.1m (1$\frac{1}{4}$yd) yellow small print fabrics (two different yellows were used)
• 1.2m (1$\frac{1}{3}$yd) pink small print fabrics (two different pinks were used)
• 60cm ($\frac{5}{8}$yd) rust red first border fabric
• 2m (2$\frac{1}{4}$yd) pink outer border fabric
• 4.4m (5yd) large floral print for backing
• Queen size flannelette sheet or thin batting
• Thread to match with fabrics for machine piecing
• Quilting thread
• Rotary cutter, ruler and mat
• Sewing machine and general sewing supplies
• 6-7in cable stencil (optional)

Above: Barn Raising Pattern.

Below: Sew the first green logs to the centre squares and press. Place the units in a stack, right sides facing up and green strip at the bottom, ready to attach the next log.

edges of the fabric pieces line up perfectly. The block will measure 11in.

ASSEMBLY

The quilt is set out in the Barn Raising Pattern with six rows of six blocks each. Lay the blocks out as shown in the diagram.

Join the first three blocks of the first row and then join the next three blocks. Join the two halves together to form the first row. Continue in the same manner for all rows. Join half the rows together and then the other half. Finally join the two halves. This reduces the weight of the quilt for as long as possible.

BORDERS

There are only three borders on this quilt. Join two of the 3in rust red border strips. Do this twice more with the other strips to make three border strips.

Check the middle measurements of your quilt top. Use this measurement to cut one strip. Divide the top edge of the quilt into four quarters. Do the same with the border strip. Match the pins and ease or stretch the border fabric to the quilt top. Machine in place and press.

Measure the middle of the quilt to include the border and cut two, 3in strips to this latest measurement. As before, divide the edges of the quilt top and the border strips into quarters and, matching pins, attach to the sides of the quilt. Press well.

The pink second border is attached in the same way using the 7in strips. Measure through the middle of the quilt as before and cut border strips to these measurements. Divide the sides of the quilt and border strips into quarters, match pins, sew and press.

QUILTING

The maker of this antique quilt did not use wadding. It appears that a sheet was used to create a very light, summer quilt. You could use a flannelette sheet or if you prefer wadding then Hobbs Poly Down would be a good choice.

Cut the backing fabric and rejoin to make a piece just larger than the quilt top. Sandwich the three layers together and baste ready for quilting. There is very little quilting on this quilt. The logs have all been quilted in the ditch between each log. The border has been quilted in a cable design going over the two border fabrics. A similar effect could be achieved using a 6-7in cable stencil from your local quilt shop.

BINDING

The maker did not bind this quilt. The fabric on the top was taken over to the back and folded under $1/4$in and finished with a slip stitch.

As binding gives a stronger finish to a quilt (it wears better) it would be advisable to add a binding. Refer to one of the other quilts featured for binding instructions.

Right: Place all the strips in the order in which they are to be attached.

Below: The completed Log Cabin block.

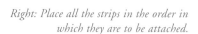

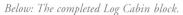

Razzle Dazzle

Susan Murphy has designed this bright quilt in a manner similar to a Log Cabin. The piecing is worked around a central shape and, as the logs are added, more corners are created so the work does not become ungainly or unbalanced. This process is a great way to use up scraps from previous projects or to show off a chosen selection that contains a wide range of colours and values.

FINISHED BLOCK SIZE

• 25cm (10in) square

FINISHED QUILT SIZE

• 198cm x 150cm (78in x 59in)

MATERIALS

• 50cm (½yd) novelty fabric for the centre blocks (enough to cut out 24 picture patches)

• 6m (6⅝yd) total of a selection of fabrics for piecing the blocks and second border

• 1.5m (1⅝yd) fabric for first and third borders

• 80cm (⅞yd) calico for foundation piecing of second border

• 216cm x 165cm (85in x 65in) piece of backing fabric

• 216cm x 165cm (85in x 65in) piece of batting

• Rotary cutter, ruler and cutting board

• 6½in x 12½in quilter's ruler

• Sewing machine in good working order

• Sewing thread in a colour to match the tone of your quilt

• General sewing requirements

• Work wall or a sheet to pin the work to

NOTE: If purchasing fabric for piecing of the blocks and second border, where possible buy 10cm (⅛yd) of as many fabrics as possible. Include bright and breezy fabrics as well as more bland ones, it is the combination of all these elements that gives your piece the extra pizzazz that these quilts offer. Fabric requirements are based on 112cm (44in) wide fabric, prewashed and ironed.

CUTTING

From the width of the calico, cut:
– six, 3½in strips. Piece them together to create two strips, 70in long and two strips, 55in long.

From the width of the first and third border fabric, cut:
– seven, 2in strips
– eight, 5in strips.

From your variety of selected fabrics for the pieced blocks and second border, cut:
– strips in a variety of lengths and widths.
– enough 2½in strips, cut on the straight of the grain, to create a length of 320in when joined together for the binding.

PREPARATION

From the novelty fabric cut 24 picture patch with a minimum of five sides to each shape. The sides should be irregular in length and no two shapes should look the same. From your assorted piecing fabrics, select and stitch a small piece of fabric to one side of the picture shape. Press the seam open and trim to suit your requirements. Refer to diagrams 1a and 1b. Turn the shape anticlockwise and add a new strip of a different fabric to the next side. Refer to diagram 2. Continue working around the shape in this manner incorporating as many different fabrics in each block as you can. Refer to diagrams 3-5. The secret with this type of block is to mix your fabrics as much as possible, to use wild and wacky combinations and under no circumstances to coordinate your choices. Spontaneity in your choices and combinations is what will create the razzle dazzle.

Remember to create more corners as you cut after adding each piece to the block. This will utilise smaller pieces in your scrapbag and also eliminate large pieces in the block, which can tend to become dominant thus loosing the lovely mix that flows through this type of quilt. Using your rotary cutter and 6½in x 12½in ruler for cutting will help to ensure your next seam line has a straight edge to follow. It is important to make all seam lines ¼in and that both raw edges are level so you are sure they are both well secured. Making this quilt is fun as there are no seams to match, but it is a difficult problem to rectify seams that have come apart because of an insufficient seam allowance.

As you work, it becomes apparent that you can work on several blocks at one time which allows you to string piece. Susan divides her blocks into manageable groups, working on six blocks at a time – piecing, cutting and pressing each addition as she goes. In this way the work seems to progress much quicker and at the end of each set of blocks you will have a significant accomplishment.

Pressing after the addition of each new piece is important, however, take care not to distort edges that are on the bias or cut off the grain. The main thing to remember is to press not iron. Each piece added increases the size of the block and working in rotation around the centre picture does not necessarily mean that when the block is finished the picture will be in the centre. This does not matter as it adds interest if some blocks are off-centre.

Continue piecing, pressing and cutting around each block until it is 11in square. You will need to add individual pieces to the corners so that the block can be made into the required square shape. Remember to press the blocks well and trim them to the required 10½in square.

ASSEMBLY

When all 24 blocks are completed arrange them on a work wall, in four rows of six blocks each, so you can see the overall effect you are creating. This is important because if you do not take the time to stand back and view your quilt it is possible to end up with a large collection of one particular colour in one area of the quilt.

When you are pleased with your arrangement, join the blocks together in rows and then join the rows to form your quilt top. Alternate the direction of your seams in each row so that as you complete the final seams they will mesh and fit together well. Press the completed pieced top well.

PIECED BORDER

From your piecing fabrics cut four irregular shapes and pin one in the centre of each of the four, 3½-in-wide calico strips. Begin piecing to these irregular shapes from your selection of fabrics. As you piece, stitch through both the arranged fabric and the calico strip. Press the applied fabric open and trim again to create more corners. Trimming will need to be done with scissors, taking care not to cut the calico foundation. Continue piecing along the entire length of all four strips. Press well and neaten any excess fabric from the calico to create strips that are 3½in wide.

BORDERS

Join the 2in strips of first border fabric. Measure your pieced top through the centre lengthwise. Cut off two strips to

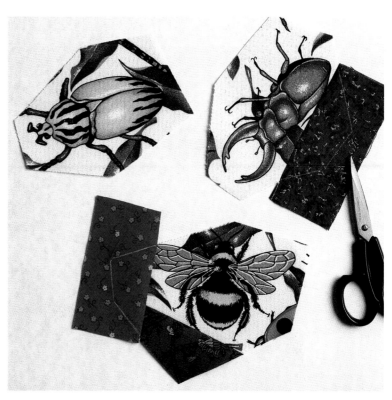

Above: Beginning with your centre picture patch, add logs one at a time, piecing, pressing and then cutting to create more corners.

Below: The top sample shows the block after one round of logs have been added while the lower sample has two rows of logs attached.

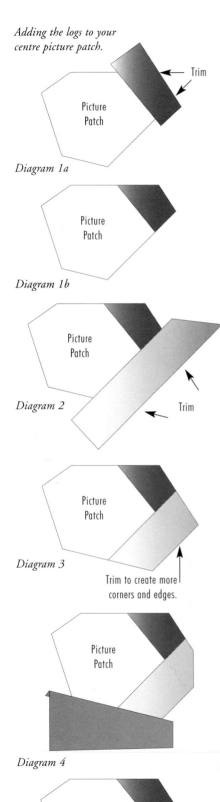

Adding the logs to your centre picture patch.

Trim

Picture Patch

Diagram 1a

Picture Patch

Diagram 1b

Picture Patch

Diagram 2

Trim

Picture Patch

Diagram 3

Trim to create more corners and edges.

Picture Patch

Diagram 4

Picture Patch

Diagram 5

this measurement. Attach these strips to the sides of the quilt and press the borders open.

Measure through the centre across the width of the quilt and cut another two, 2in strips to this measurement. Attach these to the top and bottom of the quilt. Repeat this measuring process for the strips of pieced border you created on the calico. Measure precisely and attach the strips to the sides and then the top and bottom of the quilt top.

Join the 5in-wide strips of border fabric to create the third and final border, and measure and attach as before.

QUILTING

❖

Lay your backing fabric right side down on a work surface, carefully spread your batting on top and then the quilt top, right side up. Ensure you have no buckles, tucks or pleats in the three layers and then pin or tack the three layers together in a grid fashion across the entire quilt. The more secure these layers are the easier it will be to quilt.

Susan chose to work a small stipple close to the fish shape in the centre of each block so it would stand out and

then meandering frond type shapes in the remainder of the block to create a seaweed effect. The borders were ditch stitched and accentuated with lines $1/4$in from the edges to accentuate the pieced border.

BINDING

❖

Stitch together, on a 45-degree angle, all the $2^{1}/_{2}$in binding strips. Press the seams open, then fold the strip in half lengthwise, wrong sides together. Attach the binding strip to the edges of the quilt with a generous $1/4$in seam. Mitre the corners as you come to them.

Trim away the excess batting and backing, leaving an excess of approximately $1/8$in – $1/4$in which will be folded over in the binding as you turn it to the back of your quilt and invisibly blind stitch it in place. The small excess of batting and backing helps to fill out the binding, adding to its longevity. As the binding is one of the first places to show wear, a full binding keeps its shape and repels wear better than a flat and creased edge.

Create a label for your masterpiece and attach it to the back of your quilt. ✳

A completed block ready to be trimmed back to a $10^{1}/_{2}$in square.

Decorative Dazzle

Clancy's Coverlet

This beautiful quilt, designed and made by Carolyn Swart, would be charming gracing any bed or sunny sofa. Carolyn has used her own hand-painted fabrics for the appliqué pieces to make the quilt come alive with colour.

CUTTING

Strips, squares and rectangles are all cut from the fabric's length.

From the gold fabric, cut:

– two, 5½in x 56in border strips

– two, 5½in x 49in border strips

– six, 18in squares.

You may wish to cut all the blocks and borders slightly larger to begin with to allow for appliqué shrinkage and then trim them to size later.

From the cerise fabric, cut:

– nine, 2in x 16½in sashing strips

– four, 2in x 37in sashing strips

– two, 2in x 51in outer strips

– two, 2in x 65in outer strips

– for the binding, cut as many 2½in wide strips as necessary to fit the quilt top plus an extra 12in for mitring the corners and joining.

From the pink/grey floral border fabrics, cut:

– two, 6in x 68½in strips

– two plain grey 4in x 62½in strips.

PREPARATION

From the design outline for the centre blocks shown on the pattern sheet, trace the flowers, leaves, stems and vase outlines onto template material and cut out.

Fold the gold fabric blocks in half twice to find the centre. Mark a small centre cross with blue water erasable pen and trace the pattern from the pattern sheet onto the fabric.

Each block has three large flowers and one small one. Each border has small flowers. In all there are 18 large flowers, 40 small flowers, 74 leaves, six long stems, 12 short stems, 58 flower centres and six vases.

With a lead pencil trace the required number of shapes onto iron-on interfacing,

leaving a generous ½in space between each one. Place the interfacing, shiny side down onto the wrong side of the fabric. Set your iron to cotton, turn off steam and fuse the two pieces together. Cut out each shape on the pencil line.

To avoid confusion, separate the large flowers from the small ones and the long stems from the short.

For each side border cut a strip of paper from the roll 5½in x 56in. Fold the strip in half lengthwise and from end to end and mark the centre with a cross. Trace the border pattern from the pattern sheet onto the strip.

For the top and bottom borders cut a strip 5½in x 49in and repeat as for the side borders.

On thin cardboard trace and cut out circles for the flower centres. On the wrong side of the fabric, trace around the cardboard circles with a pencil. Cut out leaving a ¼in seam allowance. Sew a running stitch around each circle just inside the allowance. Place the cardboard circles in the centre of the fabric and draw up the thread. Press each circle flat and gently remove the cardboard.

APPLIQUE

Before starting to appliqué with machine satin stitch, it is a good idea to test out the stitching on scraps of the same fabric you will be using. The stitches need to be close and flat. Do not have a ridge. Attach the embroidery foot to your machine and set it to satin stitch or a very close zigzag. Set the stitch width to 2 and length between zero and 1. This may vary with

FINISHED BLOCK SIZE

• 40.5cm (16in)

FINISHED SIZE

• 150cm x 185½cm (59in x 73in)

MATERIALS

• 2.3m (2½yd) gold-coloured fabric for blocks and borders

• 1.85m (2yd) grey and pink floral border print for outer borders

• 1.9m (2⅛yd) cerise sateen fabric for sashings, outer strips and binding

• 35cm (⅜yd) salmon-pink print for vases

• 60cm (⅝yd) hydrangea-coloured fabric for flowers

• 30cm (⅓yd) green and black stripe fabric for leaves and stems

• 15cm (⅛yd) hot pink fabric for flower centres

• 4m (4⅜yd) gold-coloured brushed heavy cotton for backing

• 4m x 120cm (4⅜yd x 47in) Pellon for batting

• 2m (2¼yd) iron-on interfacing

• Blue water-erasable pen

• Black fine-tip permanent marker

• Sharp lead pencil

• Roll of unwaxed paper

• Thin cardboard and Template material

• Rotary cutter, ruler and mat

• Sharp appliqué scissors

• Sewing machine able to drop feed dogs and do satin stitch

• ¼in machine foot, embroidery foot and darning foot

• 11/80 machine needles

• Appliqué needles

• Matching thread for flowers, leaves, stems, vases and centres

• Matching thread for quilting background fabric and sashings

• Monofilament thread

Above: Trace the appliqué shapes onto iron-on interfacing, fuse to the fabric and cut out each shape.

Below: Before stitching the vase, centre the small flower at the top of the vase and pin in place.

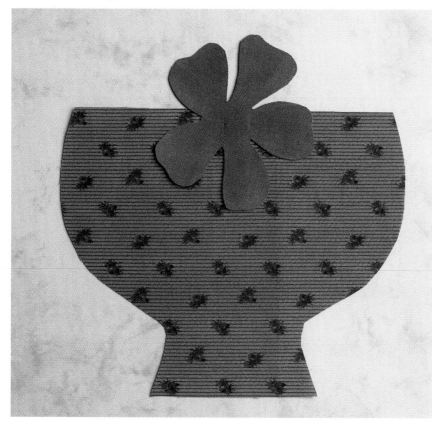

Note: All measurements are based on 112cm (44in) wide cotton fabric. A $\frac{1}{4}$in seam allowance included except where stated. Wash and iron all fabrics before use. This quilt was machine appliquéd using satin stitch. All flower centres are hand appliquéd. Borders are appliquéd first and joined to the quilt later. The end flowers on each side border, and the pair of leaves on each end of the top and bottom borders are appliquéd after all the borders have been attached.

different machines so it is important to test first. If the usual tension is 4, lower it to 3. If bobbin thread shows through on the top stitching adjust the tension.

BLOCKS

On the prepared traced blocks, position the centre and side stems first. Pin or baste and, with matching thread, satin-stitch each side of the stems. Position and pin the leaves and carefully stitch around each. Place the vase next, just covering the ends of the stems and pin or baste. Before stitching the vase, centre the small flower at top of the vase and pin in place. Refer to the colour photo. Match the thread and sew around the vase, changing thread to stitch the small flower. Position the three large flowers covering the tops of the stems and stitch. Place a flower centre on each flower and carefully slip-stitch all around each one. When all the blocks are finished, rinse thoroughly in cold water (not hot) to remove the blue pen. When dry, press the block and trim to a $16\frac{1}{2}$in square.

BORDERS

For the side borders pin together the paper and fabric borders, matching the centres and with blue water-erasable pen trace the pattern onto the fabric. Pin or baste each flower in place and satin-stitch each one. (Remember not to appliqué each end flower at this time.) Pin each leaf in place and stitch.

Repeat as for the side borders, remembering to leave each pair of end leaves until later when all the borders are joined to the quilt. When all the borders are finished, rinse in cold water to remove the blue pen. Dry and press. Trim the side borders to 54½in long, and the top and bottom borders to 47½in long.

QUILT ASSEMBLY

Join a 16½in cerise sashing strip to each side and centre of each pair of blocks. Join these blocks together with a 2in x 37in strip across the top, centre and bottom. Press this section carefully. Join the two side appliquéd borders, then the top and bottom appliquéd borders. Press carefully. Join a 2in x 65in cerise strip to each side, then a 2in x 51in cerise strip to the top and bottom. Now, refer to the border patterns and position each end flower on side borders and each pair of leaves on top and bottom borders and satin-stitch each one in place. It is not necessary to trace the pattern with blue water-erasable pen, just place over the pattern and pin. To each side, join the grey/pink floral border and then the top and bottom plain grey borders. Very carefully press the whole quilt top and square up the corners if necessary.

BACKING AND BATTING

Cut backing fabric in half and remove selvedges. Sew the two pieces together and press the seam open. Make sure the

Above: Satin-stitch around the flowers and leaves using matching threads.

Below: Make the flower centres by gathering fabric circles over cardboard templates.

CLANCY'S COVERLET
Design outline for placement of leaves at
the ends of the top and bottom borders.

backing measures 2-3in larger all around
than the quilt top. Cut and join Pellon batting
to the same size as the backing fabric.

QUILTING

Layer the backing fabric, wrong side up,
batting and quilt top. Smooth out any
wrinkles and baste together in a 3-4in
grid all over. Make sure your machine is
clean and free from lint and use a new
needle. Attach the darning foot and drop
the feed dogs. Thread the machine with
thread to match the gold background
fabric and start the stipple quilting in the
centre blocks, then the top blocks and
the bottom ones. Stipple very close to
each appliqué shape or if preferred,
outline them separately. Change thread
to match the sashing strips and stipple
each one. Quilt the side appliquéd
borders next then the top and bottom
appliquéd borders. Change the thread
again and quilt the outer cerise strips
in the same order. To quilt the outer
grey border, change thread to
monofilament and stipple each border as
before. Stitch in the ditch around each
flower centre and quilt diagonal lines
across each vase.

BINDING

Join all the binding strips together, press
seams open and fold the binding in half
wrong sides together and press. Trim the
backing and batting leaving a scant ¼in to
the edge of the quilt. Attach the ¼in foot
and raise the feed dogs on your machine.
Join the binding to the front of the quilt,
mitring the corners. Turn the binding to
the back of the quilt and with matching
thread carefully slip-stitch all around. ✳

TIPS

• When undecided about matching the thread for machine satin stitching, always choose a colour a fraction darker rather than lighter.

• When stitching with monofilament thread, always use ordinary thread in the bobbin.

• Stipple quilting uses a lot of thread so it's a good idea to wind a few bobbins at the one time.

• Always clean your machine, so it is lint free, before you start your work. Even a small amount of fluff can cause havoc with satin stitching.

Harlequin

A kaleidoscope of bright fabrics and easy machine-piecing techniques have been cleverly combined by Michelle Marvig in this striking bed-sized quilt. Made with Nine and Four Patch units the design lends itself to an infinite number of possible colour combinations.

CUTTING

From the gold fabric, cut:

– 18, 3½in strips and crosscut 140, 5in rectangles for the background.

From the orange fabric, cut:

– three, 2in strips for the centre of the Nine Patch

– one, 3⅜in strip and crosscut into five, 3⅜in squares. Cut the squares along both diagonals to yield 20 triangles used in the edge blocks. From the balance of the strip cut two, 2in squares. Cut these squares along one diagonal to yield four triangles for the corner blocks

– seven, 1in strips for the inner border.

From the purple fabric, cut:

– 21, 2in strips. From three strips crosscut 58, 2in squares for the edge triangles. The remaining 18 strips are for the Four Patch and Nine Patch blocks

– one, 3⅜in strip. Crosscut five, 3⅜in squares. Cut these squares along both diagonals to yield 20 quarter square

triangles, which are to be used in the pieced, edge triangles

– eight, 6½in strips for the outer border

– eight, 2¼in strips for the binding.

From the blue fabric, cut:

– 14, 2in strips. From two of these strips crosscut 22, 2in squares for the edge triangles.

The remaining 12 strips are for the Four Patch and Nine Patch blocks, cut:

– one, 3⅜in strip. Crosscut into 12, 3⅜in squares. Cut these squares along both diagonals to yield 48 quarter triangles for the pieced, edge triangles.

From the aqua fabric, cut:

– seven, 2in strips. From one strip crosscut eight, 2in squares for the edge triangles. The remaining six strips are for the Nine Patch blocks

– one, 3⅜in strip. Crosscut this strip into seven, 3⅜in squares. Cut these squares along both diagonals to yield 28 quarter square triangles for the pieced, edge triangles.

Diagram 1

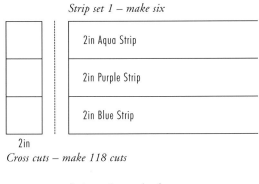

Strip set 1 – make six

2in Aqua Strip

2in Purple Strip

2in Blue Strip

2in
Cross cuts – make 118 cuts

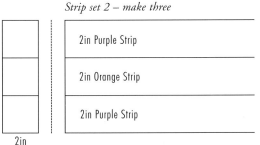

Strip set 2 – make three

2in Purple Strip

2in Orange Strip

2in Purple Strip

2in
Cross cuts – make 59 cuts

Diagram 2a
Construction of Large
Edge Triangle

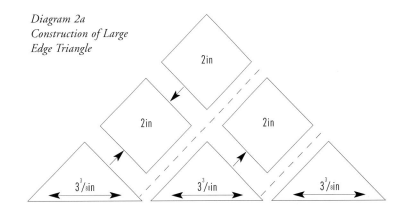

Diagram 2b

Make 12

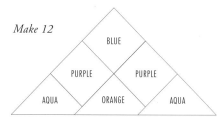

Make 8

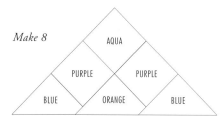

Diagram 3
Small Edge Triangles

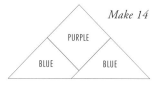

Make 14

Make 10

Diagram 4
Corner Blocks

Make 2

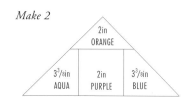

NINE PATCH BLOCKS

Two strip variations are required to make the Nine Patch blocks. Refer to diagram 1. To make Strip Set 1, stitch a purple strip between a 2in aqua strip and a 2in blue strip. Press the seams towards the purple strip in the middle. Make a total of six Strip Set 1. From these strips crosscut 118, 2in intervals.

To make Strip Set 2, stitch a 2in orange strip between two, purple strips. Press the seams towards the purple outer strips. Make a total of three Strip Set 2. From these strips crosscut 59, 2in intervals.

To complete the Nine Patch blocks, take two crosscut sections from Strip Set 1 and stitch these on either side of a crosscut section from Strip Set 2. The aqua squares should be on opposite corners of the block, the blue squares on the remaining corners. Press the seams away from the middle strip. Make a total of 59 Nine Patch blocks.

FOUR PATCH BLOCKS

Take six, 2in strips of both the purple and the blue fabrics. Stitch each purple strip to a blue strip and press the seams towards the purple. From the paired strips crosscut 116, 2in intervals. Stitch the crosscut portions back together, with the purple squares on opposite corners, to form Four Patches. Press the seam. Make a total of 58, Four Patch blocks.

EDGE TRIANGLES

There are 20 larger edge triangles and 24 smaller edge triangles. The larger edge triangles are a half Nine Patch block,

while the smaller triangles are half a Four Patch block. The colour combinations in the blocks change depending on which side of the quilt the edge triangle is for. Four corner blocks are also required.

Referring to diagrams 2a and 2b, make the large edge triangles first; using 2in squares and 3³⁄₈in quarter square triangles. The arrows in the diagrams show the pressing direction of the seams. Make eight of one combination and 12 of the other.

Referring to diagram 3, make the smaller edge triangles using only blue and purple 2in squares and 3³⁄₈in quarter square triangles. You will make 10 with blue squares and 14 with purple squares.

Make the corner triangles referring to diagram 4. Only two of each corner combination are required.

QUILT ASSEMBLY

The quilt blocks are laid out on point, with the Nine Patch and Four Patch blocks alternating. Starting with a Nine Patch block on the corner, the quilt is constructed of 13 rows of nine blocks.

Following the quilt photo on page 51, place the blocks in the quilt. The gold 3¹⁄₂in x 5in rectangles fill in the areas between the blocks. The pieced, edge triangles fill in around the edge, but be sure to keep them in the correct position. It should be as if the square blocks have been sliced in half along a diagonal, so that you are only seeing the first half of the block. The corner triangles represent only a quarter of the block.

For ease of construction, the quilt is stitched in diagonal rows. One row consists of only Nine Patch and gold rectangles, with large edge triangles on the ends of the rows. The alternate rows are made from Four Patch blocks and gold rectangles with small edge triangles on the edges of the rows. Press all seam allowances towards the gold rectangles. Once the rows are complete, stitch the rows together to make the inner portion of the quilt. Straighten the edges if required, but do not trim away the seam allowance.

BORDERS

Measure the length of your quilt. Michelle suggests measuring in three different places and recording the average of these measurements.

The inner border on the quilts is made from the 1in orange strips. Join two strips together for either side border and cut to your average measurement. Stitch onto the sides of the quilt top. Press towards the orange border. Join the remaining three strips together.

Measure the width of the quilt, and cut two strips that equal your average width from the joined strips. Stitch these to the top and bottom of the quilt top. Press towards the orange border.

Repeat this process for the outer border using the 6$\frac{1}{2}$in purple strips, stitching the sides first followed by the top and bottom. Press all seams towards the purple.

QUILTING

Cut the backing fabric into two, 2.5m lengths. Using a wide seam allowance, join down the selvedge edge. Trim off the selvedge and press the seam to one side.

Michelle machine-quilted her quilt. Before making the quilt sandwich, she marked small and large circles around the Nine and Four Patch blocks. Simple kitchen utensils such as plates can be

Above: Make each Nine Patch block by attaching a crosscut section from Strip Set 1 to either side of a crosscut section from Strip Set 2.

Below: Make the Four Patch blocks by joining crosscut sections of paired purple and blue fabric strips, with the purple squares on opposite corners.

Alternative colour variations are shown in quilts made by two of Michelle's students.

used for this purpose. These circles were continued out into the border, with a row of echo-quilted half circles completing the design.

Layer the backing fabric wrong side up, batting and well pressed quilt top. Baste the three layers together in your preferred method.

Quilt as desired. Michelle stitched in the ditch around each of the Nine and Four Patch blocks. This is easily done in diagonal rows. Then quilt the circles in the gold background fabric using a gold-coloured thread, stopping at the border. The circles in the border are stitched using a purple thread.

BINDING

To make the binding, stitch the eight, 2 $\frac{1}{4}$in wide strips of purple into one long length with 45-degree angle seams. Press the length of the binding in half, wrong sides together. Using a $\frac{1}{4}$in seam, stitch the binding around the edges of the quilt, with all raw edges even and mitring each corner. Trim the excess batting and backing fabric back to approximately $\frac{1}{4}$in beyond the edge of the quilt. Roll the binding over to the back of the quilt and hand-stitch in place. Add a label to your quilt.   ✳

Victorian Floral Reflections

Michele Hill's love of William Morris and medieval designs came about after a visit to the Victoria and Albert Museum in London. This particular design was inspired by a William Morris embroidery titled 'The Strawberry Thief'.

PREPARATION

❖

Trace the images that require a mirror image (as shown on the pattern sheet) by tracing from the reverse side of the pattern. You can do this by holding the pattern sheet up to a light source, such as taping it to a window or over a light box.

CUTTING

❖

All strips are cut across the fabric width.

From the background fabric, cut:
– one piece 30in x 39in.

From the first border fabric, cut:
– four, 2½in strips.

From the second border fabric, cut:
– four, 1in strips.

From the third border fabric, cut:
– five, 4in strips.

From the binding fabric, cut:
– five, 2½in strips.

APPLIQUE

❖

Trace all the appliqué shapes from the pattern sheet and your mirror-image shapes onto the paper side of the fusible webbing, leaving at least ½in between each shape. Use the photo of the quilt as a guide to help you with the images required. Remember that the images you have traced will be reversed when you appliqué them to the quilt so make sure you have one of each of the appropriate flowers, leaves or birds facing to the left and one to the right.

When tracing the images, take note of the dotted lines where a mirror image of the completed shape will be required, for example, the main flower at the top of the design needs to be joined on the dotted line when tracing.

Roughly cut around each shape (not on the traced line at this stage) and, using a hot iron, apply each shape to the wrong side of your chosen fabrics. When the shapes are ironed on, cut them out again, this time on the traced line.

Trace out the bird body in one piece. Trace wing, legs and beak separately and place over the top of the body. Use an appliqué mat to assemble the pieces and transfer them to the background fabric.

FINISHED QUILT SIZE

107cm x 130cm (42in x 51in)

MATERIALS

• 90cm (1yd) navy background fabric

• 30cm (⅓yd) green fabric for leaves

• 30cm (⅓yd) pale blue fabric for ferns

• 20cm (¼yd) each of the following fabrics; red for strawberries, orange for flowers, mustard and a matching floral for main flower, cream for birds and remaining flowers, and medium blue for small five-petal flowers

• 30cm (⅓yd) fabric for first border

• 20cm (¼yd) fabric for second border

• 60cm (⅔yd) fabric for third border

• 40cm (½yd) fabric for binding

• 1m (1⅛yd) fusible webbing

• 120cm x 150cm (47in x 59in) piece of backing fabric and batting

• Rayon machine embroidery thread in matching colours

• Open-toed appliqué foot for machine

• Appliqué mat

• Fine, black permanent marking pen

• 4 small seed beads for birds' eyes

• General sewing supplies

• Cotton thread in matching colours

• Blanket or design wall

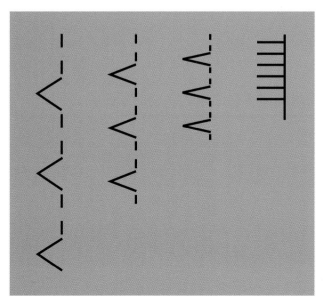

Diagram 1
Adjusting blind hemstitch to create a mock blanket stitch.

Position the bird's body, wing, beak and legs on the appliqué mat and iron as a whole piece. Peel the bird off the mat and position on the background fabric.

Before ironing the shapes into place it is recommended that the background be laid out on a blanket on the floor, or on a design wall, and all the shapes be laid out to ensure that they fit.

Be careful not to spread out the appliqué too far or it may not fit. If you look closely at the photo, you will see that most of the pieces touch each other. Be particularly careful not to spread out the strawberry stem too wide.

When you are pleased with the positioning of all the shapes, peel the paper off the back and carefully iron each shape onto the background fabric. Take particular note of any pieces that need to be tucked under other shapes. Use the quilt photo and the numbering shown on the photo as a guide.

TIP BOX
USING AN APPLIQUE MAT

Appliqué mats are available from quilt supply outlets. They are made from teflon so fusible webbing will not stick to them.

They are particularly useful for assembling shapes made up of a number of small pieces such as the birds in this design.

Place the appliqué mat over your pattern. Assemble all the parts of the bird using the pattern, which will show through the mat, as a guide. When you are sure of the position of all the pieces, iron them together as a whole piece. The assembled bird can then be peeled off the mat and appliquéd to the quilt top.

Trace out the bird body in one whole piece. Trace the wing, legs and the beak separately and place over the top of the body. Use an appliqué mat to assemble the pieces and then transfer them to the background fabric.

EMBROIDERY

❖

Appliqué around each shape using blanket stitch. This can be done by hand, but Michele prefers to do hers by machine using a rayon machine embroidery thread in the top and a matching cotton thread in the bobbin. All threads should match the appliqué pieces. If your machine does not have a blanket stitch, try adjusting the width and length of the blind hemstitch (if possible) to achieve a mock blanket stitch. Refer to diagram 1.

Draw a small black circle for each bird's eye, using a fine, permanent marking pen. Stitch a small bead into the centre of each circle.

BORDERS

When the appliqué is completed, attach the borders using a ¼in seam allowance.

Measure through the centre of the quilt lengthways and cut two first border strips to fit and attach to the sides of the quilt. Then measure through the centre of the quilt widthways and cut the other two strips to fit and attach.

Add the second border in the same manner. For the third border measure width and length and join strips to fit. Attach the side borders first.

Sandwich the backing fabric, batting and quilt top together and baste through the three layers.

Quilt as desired. Michele has echo quilted around each shape and quilted straight lines in the borders.

BINDING

Join, on the cross, the five, 2½in binding strips to make one long length. Press the strip in half, wrong sides together and raw edges even. Attach to the front of the quilt using a ¼in seam and mitring the corners as you come to them.

Trim back the excess backing and batting and fold binding to the back of the quilt and hand-stitch in place.

Sign and date the back of your quilt for future generations. ✳

Hearts and Diamonds

The design of this scrap quilt by Bev Darby depends on the light/dark contrast of a warm selection of fabrics. Although this quilt looks intricate, half-square triangles (and a few squares around the edge of the quilt top) make it an easy quilt to sew, but an unusual one because the hearts are only formed when the blocks are joined.

CUTTING

From the light fabrics, cut:
– 194, 3⅞in squares
– 48, 3½in squares.

From the dark fabrics, cut:
– 242, 3⅞in squares.

From the width of the first border fabric, cut:
– 1½in strips and join these to make
– 2 strips, 1½in x 66½in
– 2 strips, 1½in x 68½in.

From the length of the second border fabric, cut:
– 2 strips, 3½in x 68½in
– 2 strips, 3½in x 74½in
– 4 strips, 2½in x 81in for binding.

PREPARATION

Take the 194, 3⅞in light fabric squares and rule a diagonal line across the back of each one. Do the same with 24 of the dark fabric 3⅞in squares.

Pair the 194 light fabric 3⅞in squares with unmarked dark fabric 3⅞in squares. Pair the 24 marked dark fabric 3⅞in squares with the unmarked dark fabric squares. Place the pairs right sides together and sew ¼in seams on either side of the ruled diagonal lines. Cut along the ruled lines and then open out the new squares. Press seams towards dark fabrics. Now you will have 388 light/dark squares and 48 dark/dark squares.

FINISHED BLOCK SIZE
• 46cm (18in)

FINISHED QUILT SIZE
• 191cm (75in) square

MATERIALS
• 3m (3⅓yd) total of light-coloured print fabrics
• 3m (3⅓yd) total of dark-coloured print fabrics
• 30cm (⅓yd) fabric for first border
• 2m (2¼yd) fabric for second border and binding
• 4m (4½yd) backing fabric
• 198cm (78in) square of Nu-wool batting
• Neutral-coloured sewing thread
• Clear monofilament thread for machine quilting
• Sewing thread to match backing fabric for machine quilting
• Rotary cutter, ruler and mat
• Sewing machine, cleaned with a new No 12 needle

Note: It is suggested fabrics be 100 per cent cotton, pre-washed and ironed. Fabric requirements are based on 112cm (44in) wide fabric. All cutting measurements include a ¼in seam allowance.

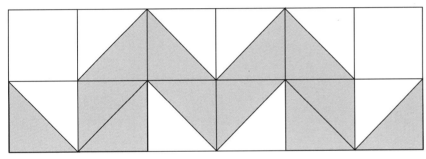

A completed Partial Block A.

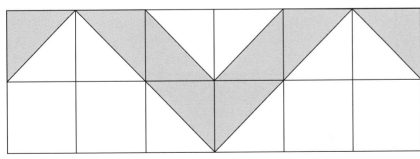

A completed Partial Block B.

A completed Partial Block D.   *A completed Partial Block C.*

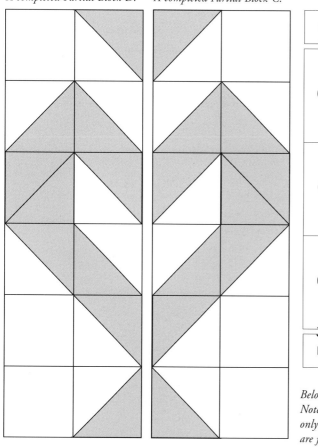

Above: Quilt Layout Diagram.

Below: A completed block. Note that heart shapes are only formed when blocks are joined.

Below: A completed Block E.

DESIGNER'S NOTE

This quilt represents much of my life. The colourful hearts represent the blessings, the joy of family and friends, health, the beauty of the garden and where I live. Also my occupation as teacher and quilt maker.

The red heart is a reminder that in every life there are sad experiences — the loss of parents, a close friend or a favourite pet.

The diamonds — the jewels of my life — symbolise wonderful events: weddings, the arrival of grandchildren and Christmas.

CONSTRUCTION

These pieced squares are then constructed into nine blocks and a variety of partial blocks.

For each of the nine main blocks, lay out 32 light/dark squares and four dark/dark squares as shown in the block diagram. Join the squares in rows and then join the rows to form each block.

Partial Block A: You need to make three of these blocks. Lay out eight light/dark, two dark/dark and two light 3½in fabric squares and assemble as shown in Partial Block A diagram.

Partial Block B: Make three of these blocks using eight light/dark and four light 3½in squares. Assemble as shown in the diagram.

Partial Blocks C and D: You will need three of each of these blocks. Each block is made up of eight light/dark, one dark/dark and three light 3½in squares. Refer to the diagrams noting the differences between the C and D blocks.

Corner Blocks E: You will need to make four corner blocks. Each block consists of one light/dark and three light 3½in squares joined as shown in the diagram.

ASSEMBLY

Join the nine main blocks together. Join the three A units together and sew these to the top of the nine units.

Join the three B units and sew these to the bottom of the centre panel. Refer to the Quilt Layout diagram.

Join the three C units and sew an E unit to both ends. These are then sewn to the left side of the quilt. Attach the remaining E units to the D units and sew to the right side of the quilt.

Above: Completed Block.

Below: Completed Block A and B.

Above: Completed Block C and D (on the right).

Below: Completed Block E.

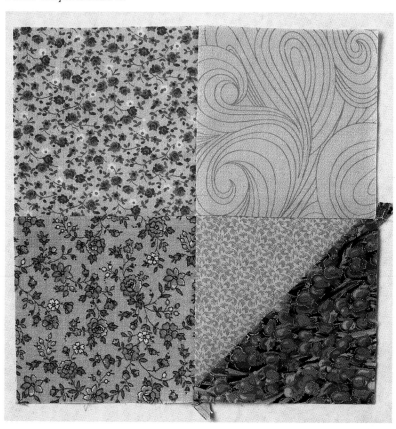

BORDERS

Sew the two shorter inner border strips to the sides of the quilt and then the longer strips to the top and bottom.

Repeat this process for the outer border, sewing the shorter strips to the sides of the quilt first and then the longer strips to the top and bottom of the quilt.

BACKING

Cut the length of backing fabric in half, remove the selvedges and join the two pieces to make a backing a little larger than the quilt top, with one vertical join.

Layer the backing, batting and quilt top and pin or baste the three layers together.

QUILTING

Bev quilted in the ditch around the hearts and the diamonds, then in the centre of the diamonds. She also quilted in the ditch along both sides of the narrow border.

BINDING

Trim the binding and batting to ¼in beyond the quilt top. Join the 2½in binding strips together. Fold the binding strip in half, wrong sides together and aligning all the raw edges sew to the top of the quilt, mitring the corners as you come to them. Turn the folded edge of the binding to the back of the quilt and hand-stitch in place. Don't forget to sign and date the back of your quilt. ✽

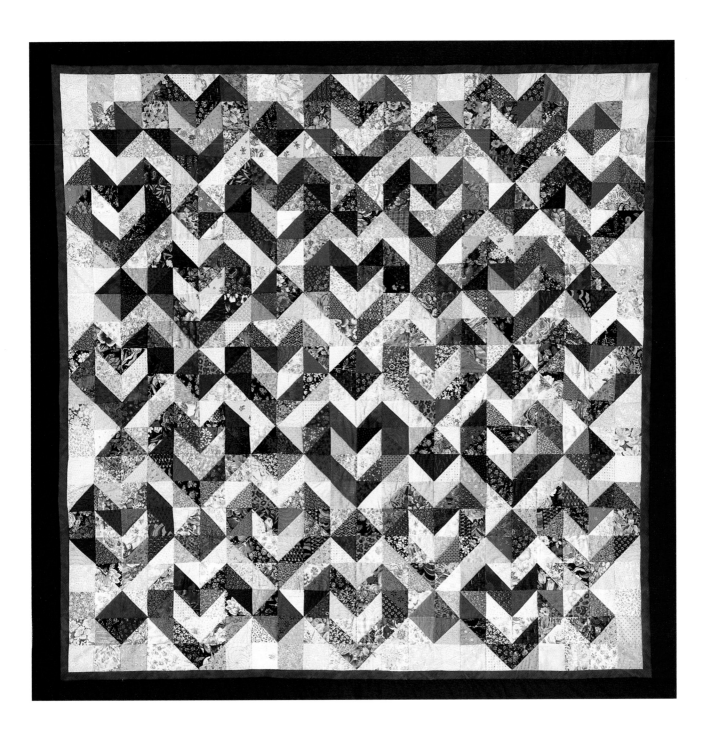

Rainbow Rails

A rainbow of brilliant colour reaches across this quilt enhanced by the sharp contrast of the black background. Showcasing vibrant hand-dyed fabrics, Val Robinson has complemented her design by machine quilting in a circular pattern to contrast with the simple linear piecing.

CUTTING

A ¼in seam allowance is included in all cutting measurements.

From each colour of hand-dyed fabric, cut:

– four, 6cm x 56cm (2¼in x 22in) strips.

From the width of the black homespun, cut:

– 25, 4cm (1½in) strips and crosscut 20, into 40, 56cm (22in) strips

– five, 14cm (5½in) strips for the border

– six, 6.5cm (2½in) strips for the binding.

PIECING

Join a short 1½in strip of black homespun to each of the 2¼in strips of hand-dyed fabric.

Press the seams to the black strips and measure across the strips to check that they are 8.5cm (3¼in) wide.

Lay all the strips on the cutting board on top of each other but with staggered seams so you can see ¼in of each fabric.

Cut across the ends to square up then crosscut at 8.5cm (3¼in) intervals six times. This method is quicker and more accurate than cutting each individual strip. You should have 24 Rail Fence blocks per colour.

ASSEMBLY

Sort the blocks into a graded arrangement of light through dark, or around the colour wheel.

Take one colour set of blocks and lay them on the Pellon, the floor or a design wall. One colour will travel across the quilt in a diagonal fashion with all its black strips horizontal. The next neighbouring colour will have its black strips sitting vertically.

Colours touch colours and black touches black, the black following through to form the steps. Refer to the colour photo. There should be 15 Rail Fence blocks down and 14 across.

When you are pleased with your arrangement, commence sewing the rows together.

Working from the top left-hand corner, flip the second vertical row onto the first vertical row and stack from the top. Chain piece the rows together in pairs. Do not cut the threads between each block or press the seam allowances at this stage.

Lay the chain-sewn blocks out again to check the sequence. Flip the fourth row of blocks onto the third row, stack and chain piece as before. Continue across the quilt in this manner.

When all the vertical rows have been joined commence sewing the horizontal rows from the top left-hand corner. Clip the chained thread between the second and third rows of blocks across the quilt. Flip the first row onto the second row. Do not clip the threads between the pairs as this keeps them in order. You will need to pin to control them. Sew across this row butting the seam allowances. As the seams are not pressed they are easy to move and to butt together. Make it a rule that the seam allowance on the top is flipped towards the needle and the one underneath is fed through easily by the machine feed dogs.

Press the seams of the four-block units and lay out the blocks again. Do not clip the threads on this row yet.

Continue onto the next horizontal row. Flip, pin, sew and press the third and fourth rows. Continue in this sequence down the quilt.

Now sew these units into eight-block units. Clip the thread between the

FINISHED BLOCK SIZE

•7cm (2¾in) square

FINISHED QUILT SIZE

•133cm x 144cms (52½in x 56½in)

MATERIALS

•2.5m (2¾yd) black homespun fabric

•Quilter's Fat Quarters – 56cm x 50cm (22in x 19in) in each of 10 hand-dyed fabrics

•3m (3¼yd) backing fabric

•150cm (59in) square of Pellon

•Black, 100 per cent cotton thread for piecing

•Smoke coloured, monofilament thread for quilting in the ditch

•Sulky variegated thread for decorative quilting

•Open-toed embroidery foot and walking foot for decorative machine quilting

•Quilter's guide machine attachment

•Rotary cutter, quilter's ruler and cutting mat

•12.5cm (5in) diameter tin lid

NOTE: Fabric should be 100 per cent cotton homespun or calico, 112cm (44in) wide.

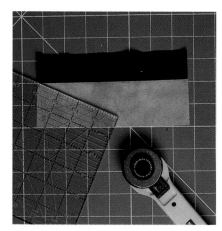

Join the strips of black homespun and hand-dyed fabrics. Check the joined strips measure 3¹/₄in across.

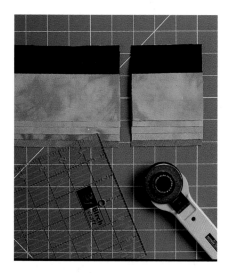

Lay all the strips on the cutting board with staggered seams and crosscut at 3¹/₄in intervals.

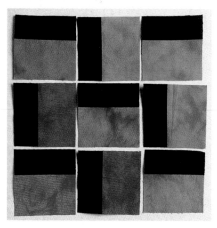

Lay out the blocks on the Pellon. Colours touch colours and black touches black.

second and third row vertically and flip, pin, sew and press. Continue joining in this manner horizontally and vertically until the quilt top is completed.

CUTTING

❖

Sew the remaining 4cm (1¹/₂in) strips of black homespun end to end and press the seams.

Measure vertically through the centre of the quilt top and cut two strips to that measurement [approximately 111.5cm (43in)]. Pin the strips to the sides of the pieced top, pinning in the centre, at each end and at the quarter points. Add more pins as necessary. When sewing, sew right up to the pin before removing it. This eases the quilt to fit and makes it lay flat and square.

Measure horizontally through the centre of the quilt [approximately 104cm (41in)] and cut two strips to that measurement. Pin and sew as before.

CHECKERBOARD BOARDER

❖

Cut your left over Rail Fence blocks in half vertically through the black and coloured strips. Arrange these in a pleasing sequence and sew them together with the black strips sitting vertically. Pin, sew and press this border to the top and bottom of the quilt.

OUTER BORDER

❖

Sew the 14cm (5¹/₂in) strips of black homespun together in one long length.

Measure the length of the quilt vertically through the centre of the quilt and cut two border strips to that measurement [approximately 121cm (48in)]. Pin, sew and press the side borders.

Measure the width of the quilt through the centre and cut the top and bottom borders to that measurement [approximately 131cm (51¹/₂in)]. Attach these borders as before.

QUILTING

❖

Cut the backing fabric in half to yield two, 150cm (59in) pieces. Cut one piece in half again lengthwise. Remove the selvedges and sew the two smaller strips to the sides of the larger piece.

Tape the backing fabric, right side down, onto a flat surface and layer the batting and pieced top on top of the backing fabric. Using stainless steel safety pins, pin the three layers together.

Stabilise the quilt first by stitching in the seam ditch along every second horizontal row using the smoke-coloured monofilament thread.

Use a lid from a tin to draw a circle at random points over the quilt. Thread the machine with variegated Sulky thread and install the quilter's guide on the machine or in the walking foot, approximately 3cm (1¹/₄in) away from the needle.

Secure the starting point by sewing up and down in the one spot four to five times, then sew around the circle. When you return to the starting point, sew at an angle until the quilter's guide touches the circle. Keep an eye on the quilter's guide resting on the sewing line and sew around like a snail's shell.

When this circle is large enough, start another circle. Where the lines meet, stop sewing by retarding the quilt and sewing up and down in the one spot four to five times.

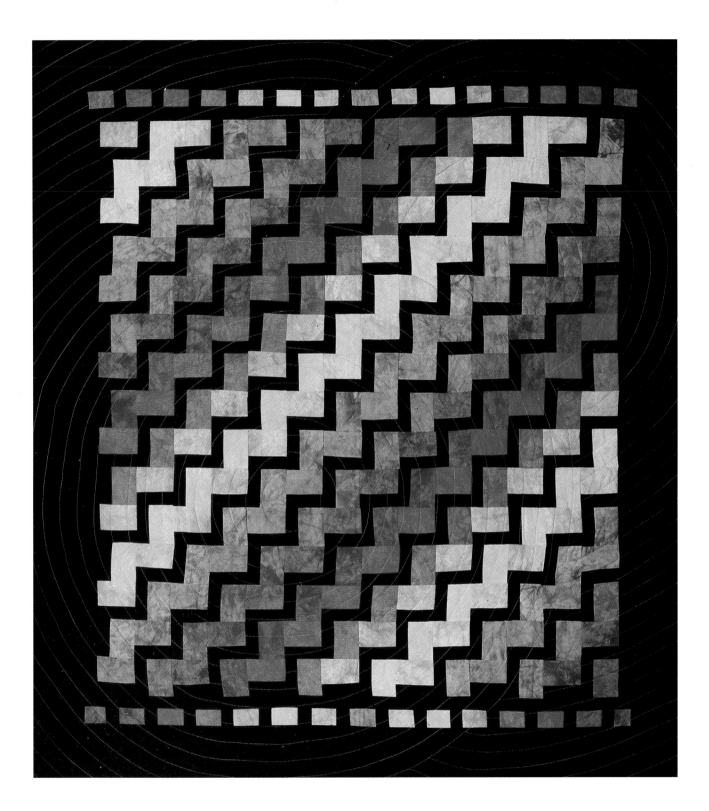

BINDING

Join the 6.5cm (2½in) lengths of binding fabric together to form one long strip. Press this in half lengthwise, with wrong sides together. With all raw edges together, stitch the binding to the front of the quilt, starting on the sides first. Trim away any excess batting or backing and roll the binding to the back of the quilt and slip-stitch in place. Attach the binding to the top and bottom of the quilt folding in the raw ends at each end. Fold to the back and slip-stitch in place.

Don't forget to sign and date your quilt.   ✳

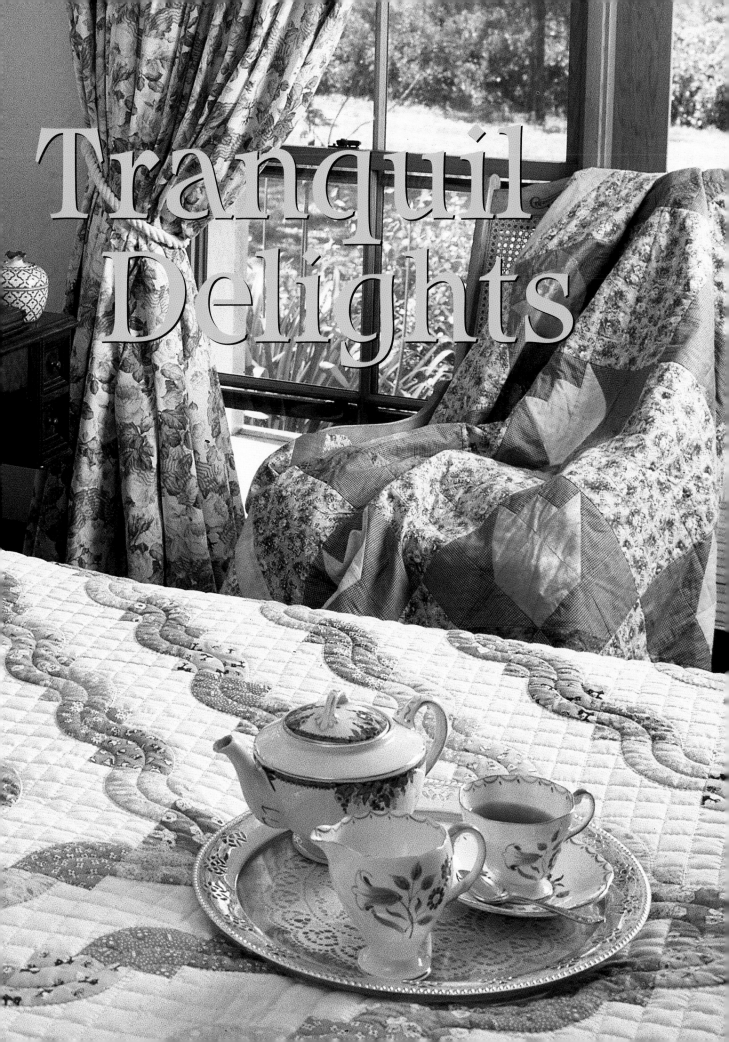

Tranquil
Delights

Emma's Flower Garden

This quilt was designed by Tracey Browning's 5¹/₂ year old daughter, Emma, using a quilting program on the family computer, with a little help from mum! Emma was so pleased with the result that mum was instructed to make this quilt for her bed, on which it now resides.

CUTTING

All cutting requirements include a ¹/₄in seam allowance. All instructions are for cutting strips across the fabric width, with the exception of the background floral fabric for the borders, alternate and setting blocks and binding.

A cutting placement guide is provided to maximise the use of your fabric for these pieces. Please read all instructions carefully before cutting.

From the blue check fabric, cut:
– four, 4¹/₂in strips, crosscut into 36, 4¹/₂in squares
– three, 4⁷/₈in strips, crosscut into 24, 4⁷/₈in squares
– two, 2¹/₂in strips, crosscut into 12, 2¹/₂in x 4¹/₂in rectangles
– with the remainder of the strip crosscut into 12, 2¹/₂in squares.

From the green print fabric for the leaves, cut:
– two, 4⁷/₈in strips, crosscut into 12, 4⁷/₈in squares.

From the pink print fabric for the flowers, cut:
– one, 4⁷/₈in strip, crosscut into six, 4⁷/₈in squares and then cut two, 4¹/₂in squares from the remainder of this strip
– cut a partial strip, 18in x 4¹/₂in and crosscut it into four, 4¹/₂in squares (you now have a total of 6, 4¹/₂in squares)
– cut another partial strip utilising the rest of the width from before, 15in x 2¹/₂in and crosscut into six, 2¹/₂in squares
– cut three, 2¹/₂in strips and put aside for the first border.

From the yellow print fabric for the flowers, cut:
– six, 4⁷/₈in, 4¹/₂in and 2¹/₂in squares as for the pink flower fabric
– four, 2¹/₂in strips and put aside for the first border.

From the background fabric, cut the alternate blocks, setting blocks and second border, referring to the cutting diagram. Cut in order as follows:

– cut the borders and six, 12¹/₂in squares from the length of the fabric. Fold the fabric lengthwise, noting the longest length required and only folding to this point. Make sure that the fabric is straight and trim the selvedge from one side. Cut the two longest borders first, 88in x 6¹/₂in

– refold carefully, straighten and cut a strip 76in x 12¹/₂in and crosscut into six, 12¹/₂in squares

– cut the top and bottom borders, 71in x 6¹/₂in

– with the remaining fabric still folded, cut a 2¹/₂in strip along the length for the binding

– open out the fabric and from the side where you cut the longest border, cut a rectangle 19in x 9¹/₂in and cut in half to create two, 9¹/₂in squares. Cut these squares once diagonally to create four, corner setting triangles

– on the other side of the fabric from this rectangle, cut an 18¹/₂in square

– lastly, fold the fabric in half, selvedge to selvedge and straighten the edge. Cut an 18¹/₂in strip and crosscut into two, 18¹/₂in squares. (You now have three, 18¹/₂in squares.) Cut these squares twice diagonally to create 12 triangles – the setting triangles on the sides of your quilt. (There will be two leftover for another project.)

– from the remaining fabric cut six, 2¹/₂in strips across the fabric for the rest of your binding.

BLOCK CONSTRUCTION

Using the quilt photo as a guide, begin by making the 12 flower blocks, six each of yellow and pink.

Diagram 1

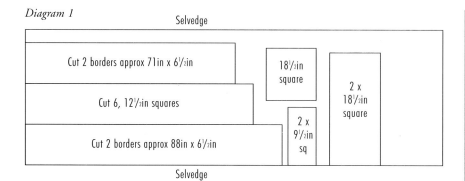

Diagram 2

Diagram 3

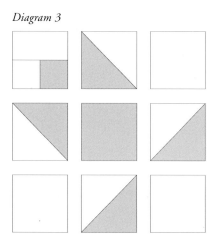

TIP

A scant $1/4$in seam is one that is one to two threads smaller than the $1/4$in. This will produce a perfect unit, as once the unit is pressed a couple of threads will be taken up in the seam fold itself.

Place right sides together,

– 12 green, $4^7/8$in squares and 12 blue check, $4^7/8$in squares

– six blue check, $4^7/8$in squares and six yellow, $4^7/8$in squares

– six blue check, $4^7/8$in squares and six pink, $4^7/8$in squares.

On the lightest fabric of each pair, draw a line from one corner to the other across the diagonal. Sew a scant $1/4$in seam on either side of this line. Repeat for all pairs of squares and then cut along the drawn line to produce two half-square units.

Press these units well and check that they all measure $4^1/2$in square, trimming the points as you go.

Next, join the 12 blue check $2^1/2$in squares to the six each of yellow and pink $2^1/2$in squares. Chain piece the blue check squares to the yellow and pink squares to make 12 units measuring $2^1/2$in x $4^1/2$in. Then join these units to the 12 blue check rectangles of the same size to form $4^1/2$in squares.

Lay out the units for each flower block in a nine-patch configuration. Join the units together to form three rows. Press the seams in each row in opposite directions. This will assist in sewing the rows together to complete the block. The finished block should measure $12^1/2$in.

Once you have completed the 12 flower blocks and pressed them well, lay out the blocks on a flat surface or a design wall alternating with the $12^1/2$in square background blocks. Note that the

TIP

To do this quickly, chain piece all the half-square triangles at the same time. Chain piecing saves on time and thread. Place your first unit under the presser foot and sew to within a couple of stitches of the end. Get your next unit and feed it under the presser foot as you continue sewing with approximately $1/8$in of thread between the units. Feed all your pairs of fabric through in one direction then turn them around and without cutting them apart, feed them through in the other direction. Once finished cut them apart and press.

blocks are placed on point. Fill in the gaps on the edges of the quilt with the quarter-square triangles cut from the $18^1/2$in squares. Finally, the half-square triangles cut from the $9^1/2$in squares fill in the corners.

Join the quilt together in diagonal rows. Press gently as you go as the top is easily stretched at this stage.

FIRST BORDER

Measure your quilt down the centre both horizontally and vertically and write these measurements down. Tracey's quilt measured 51in x 68in at this stage. Trim your four, $2^1/2$in yellow strips to $40^1/2$in. To determine the lengths needed of the pink strips, use the following formula.

The quilt has mitred corners so you need to allow for this in your measurements.

Border length plus 4in = Qin.

Qin – 40in = total pink required. Divide this by two and add $1/2$in for seam allowances. You will need to cut two lengths for each side of this measurement.

For example, Tracey's quilt worked out as follows:

Top and bottom borders,

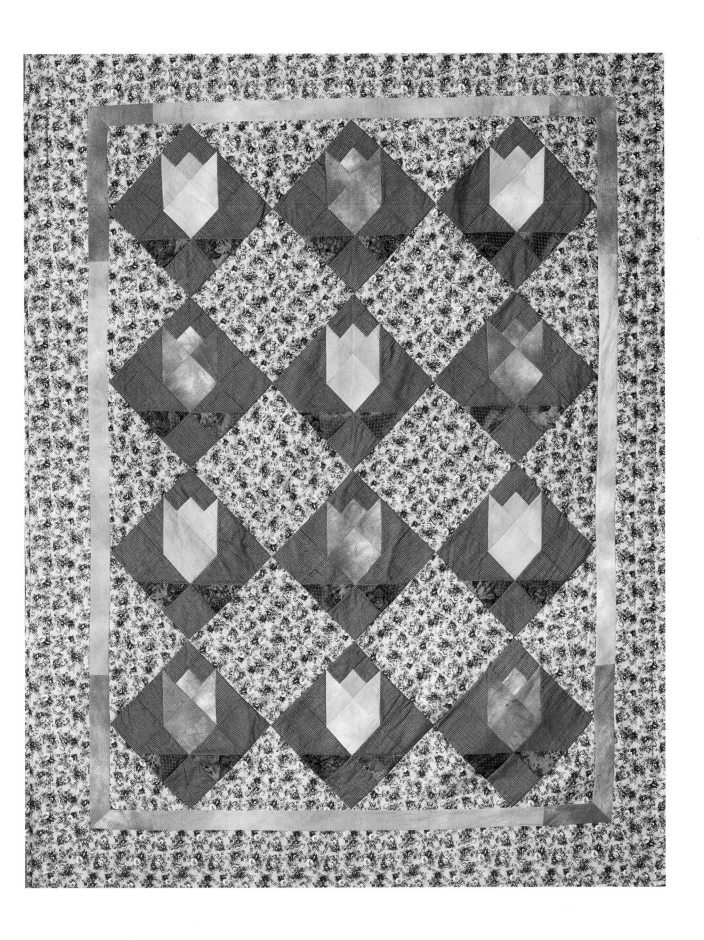

51in + 4in = 55in. 55in – 40in = 15in.
15in ÷ 2 + $\frac{1}{2}$in = 8in lengths x 4.
Side borders,
68in + 4in = 72in. 72in – 40in = 32in.
32in ÷ 2 + $\frac{1}{2}$in = 16 $\frac{1}{2}$in lengths x 4.

Insert your measurements to determine your own requirements.

With your three pink 2$\frac{1}{2}$in strips you will need to measure and cut your borders as you have calculated them. Join these to each end of the yellow strips to make them the correct length for each side. Pin, matching the quarter, half and three-quarter points on the quilt and sew to within $\frac{1}{4}$in of each end of the seam. Press the seam allowances towards the borders.

To mitre the corners, place the quilt top flat, wrong side up, lapping the border strips. At one corner, rule a 45-degree diagonal line on the upper border. Reverse the lapping to mark the underneath border strip in the same way. Fold the quilt corner on the diagonal, keeping right sides together, with edges even. Align and pin the marked lines. Stitch on the line, working from the inner corner to the outer edge. Trim the excess fabric and press.

SECOND BORDER

❖

The strips for this border are cut to the quilt's measurements, plus twice the border width.

Measure the length of the quilt top through the centre and add 12in and cut two of the longest border strips to this measurement. The length of the border should be approximately 84in.

Pin-mark the borders and the quilt top into quarters. Pin and sew the borders to the opposite sides of the quilt top, beginning and ending $\frac{1}{4}$in from the ends, securing with back stitching. Press the seams towards the borders.

Measure the width of the quilt top through the centre, add 12in and cut the remaining two border strips to this measurement which should be about 67in.

Pin, sew and press these border strips to the top and bottom of the quilt. Mitre the corners as for the first border.

QUILTING

❖

Cut the length of backing fabric in half and remove the selvedges. Join the two pieces down the long sides and press the seam open.

Lay out the backing, wrong side up and smooth to remove any wrinkles, working on a large flat surface such as the floor. Tape the backing to the floor, with packing tape to carpet or masking tape to hard floors. Centre the wadding on top and smooth out from the centre. Place the well-pressed pieced top on top of the wadding and backing, and smooth out again.

Keeping the layers smooth at all times, pin-baste the quilt in a grid pattern starting from the centre and working out to the edges at a fist width or 4in intervals. If possible, place the pins in positions that will not interfere with machine quilting.

Tracey machine-quilted the alternate blocks in a 2in-grid pattern and quilted in the ditch around the flowers in the flower blocks. The border has been quilted with straight lines 2in apart all the way around, continuing on with the simple straight line quilting theme.

BINDING

❖

Sew the 2$\frac{1}{2}$in binding strips together using a 45-degree seam and press the

seams open. Press the long strip in half, wrong sides together. Align the raw edge of the binding to the front of the quilt and sew with a $\frac{1}{4}$in seam, mitring each corner. Trim the excess of the edges of the wadding and backing to $\frac{1}{4}$in from the seam line and turn the binding to the back. Slip-stitch the binding to the back using a thread to match the binding fabric.

Lastly, make a label for your quilt that includes your name, address, the date, the name of the quilt and any other relevant details. Use a permanent pen to ensure that the details do not wash away. Stitch this to your quilt so that future generations will know the creator. ✳

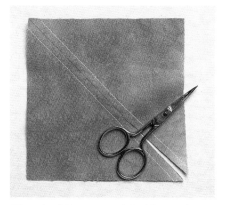

Place the 4$\frac{7}{8}$in squares right sides together, sew a scant $\frac{1}{4}$in seam on either side of the drawn diagonal line and cut along the line to create two half-square units.

Lay out the units for each flower block in a nine-patch configuration. Join the units to form three rows and join the rows to complete the block.

Tipsy Trail

After collecting this range of fabrics over a few years, Anne Perry finally decided to use it for this variation of Drunkard's Path as a gift for her daughter Emily. The fabrics conjure up lovely memories for Anne's mother who fondly recalls many of them as her own mother's dresses, clothes and nightwear from her childhood. As Anne loves hand sewing and quilting, she found the curved piecing a very rewarding activity.

FINISHED BLOCK SIZE

- 10cm (4in) square

FINISHED QUILT SIZE

- 166cm x 226cm (65½in x 89in)

MATERIALS

- 20 different fat quarters in a wide selection of colours from the 1930s reproduction range of fabrics
- 4.25m (4¾yd) of good quality cream homespun, 2m (2¼yd) for piecing and 2.25m (2½yd) for borders
- 1.5m (1⅝yd) contrast homespun for binding
- 5m (5½yd) backing fabric
- Wadding to fit size of quilt
- Neutral sewing thread for piecing
- Cream quilting thread
- Needles to suit individual taste
- Marking pencil
- Fine permanent marking pen
- Template plastic
- Sandpaper covered board
- 2.5cm (1in) wide masking tape
- General sewing requirements

Note: Pre-wash and iron all fabric. Fabric requirements are based on 112cm (44in) wide fabric.

PREPARATION

❖

Prepare templates A and B by carefully placing the template plastic over the templates provided and tracing with permanent marking pen. Remember to mark the grainline. The templates are finished size and a ¼in seam allowance must be added when cutting the fabrics.

CUTTING

❖

Using a sandpaper covered board as a base to hold the fabric in place, cut from template A, 212 pieces in a variety of colours. These are for the body of the quilt. Then cut a further 124 pieces, also in a variety of colours, from the same template and set aside for the border.

From the cream homespun, using template B, cut 212 pieces. Whilst drawing around the patterns take care to mark the tiny notches. These will help you to keep the fabric aligned when piecing the curve.

From the cream homespun also cut four, 4in squares plus a ¼in seam allowance for the quilt centre.

From the length of cream homespun for the borders cut, four strips 25cm (10in) wide.

Cut the binding fabric into 3in-wide bias strips.

PIECING CURVED SEAMS

❖

Match up in pairs, one of the 212 coloured shapes from template A with one of the 212 cream homespun shapes cut from template B.

When piecing the curved seam A to B, it is easier to work with the concave (inward) curve towards you. Take care that the marked stitching line is aligned and pinned at regular intervals matching the corner points and the centre notch.

Press the seam away from the cream to avoid the colour showing through on the quilt top.

ASSEMBLY

❖

Lay out the finished blocks, starting with the four cream centre blocks. Refer to the photograph of the quilt for placement.

Take time to balance the colours, by standing back to look at the overall effect.

Working row by row, join the blocks by machine, carefully matching the seam intersections.

BORDERS

❖

Measure the width and the length of the quilt top through the centre of the quilt for an accurate border measurement. Cut the 25cm (10in) strips to fit, allowing enough fabric for mitring. Attach top and bottom, then sides and mitre the corners. Press the seam towards the border.

The appliquéd Tipsy Trail around the border requires the other 124 coloured shapes made using template A. Join the shapes side by side, one up, one down as shown in the photograph.

After joining, press gently so as not to stretch, with the seams going in the one direction. Clip the curves and tack the curved sides ready for appliqué.

Along each border, mark a light pencil line 12cm (4¾in) out from the border seam. Use this as a guide to lay the strip of joined A pieces. They can be moved in or out to adjust to the border. Pin, baste, then appliqué the Tipsy Trail in place.

QUILTING

Remove the selvedges and cut the length of backing fabric in half. Sew the long edges together to make a quilt backing a little larger than the quilt top with one vertical seam pressed open.

Layer the well-pressed quilt top, batting and backing together. Baste well all over, about 12.5cm (5in) apart.

Starting in the centre, quilt in a grid, using the 1in masking tape, on the cream areas. This creates an overall grid pattern as the seam lines blend away. The coloured areas are quilted with three curved lines, 1in apart, following the curve of the pieces. These lines flow from one piece to another.

Quilt the border with lines 1in apart, which join to the grid pattern. These lines begin at the border seam line and continue out to the border appliqué.

The Tipsy Trail around the border also has the three curved lines quilted, flowing from one to the other. The last three rows on the outer edge of the border are quilted 1in apart on the cream, echoing the Tipsy Trail. Refer to the photo as a guide. Trim the edges of the quilt in preparation for the binding. Shape the corners of the quilt by curving off the point.

BINDING

Join the strips together with a bias seam and press open. Fold strip in half, wrong sides together, then press. Beginning half way along one side of quilt, sew the binding to the front of quilt. When going around the corners, pin the binding at regular intervals so it will lay flat. Turn the binding over to the back of the quilt and slip-stitch the folded edge into place. Remember to sign and date your quilt. ✳

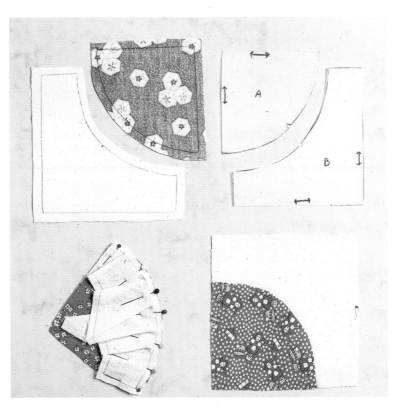

Above: Match up the A and B pairs for each block. It is easier to work with the concave curve towards you when piecing the curved seam.

Below: Press the seam away from the cream to avoid the colour showing through. Join the blocks row by row matching the seam intersections.

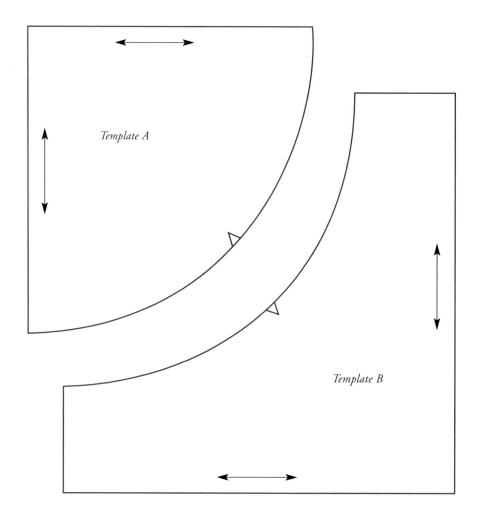

Template A

Template B

Below: Join the coloured shapes for the border appliqué, press gently and tack the curved sides ready for attaching to the border strips.

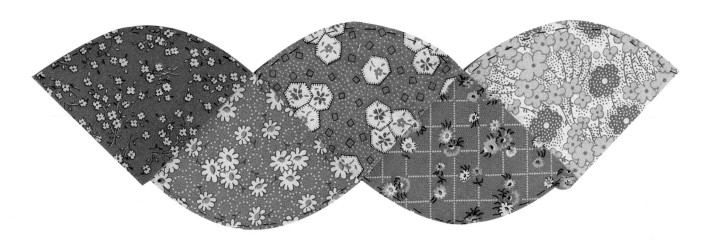

Four Doves Cushion

Use up some of your colourful scraps to make these fun, decorative cushions designed by Margaret Cormack. Either use the template to centre a special design in the large parallelogram shapes or just cut the shapes from strips, varying the colours to suit your décor.

CUTTING

Note: It is important for accurate piecing that the strips and squares be cut using the imperial measurements given here. All seam allowances are ¼in and all fabrics are cut across the full width of the fabric.

Sew the two full 1½in strips together. Press the seam in the one direction. Sew the star-point strip to the first half of the other strips. Press well.

Fold the strip in half and cut a 45-degree angle at the end. Make eight cuts at this angle, 1½in apart, each cut producing two pieces.

One piece should slope to the right and one to the left as shown in diagram 1.

If using the 2½in strip for the large parallelogram, (units 2 and 4) cut a 45-degree angle at one end and then cut four, 2½in sections from each fabric.

CUSHION TOP

❖

Lay out the pieces as shown in the Block Assembly Diagram. Referring to the numbers on the block diagram, sew 1 to 2 and 3 to 4. Press the seam towards the large parallelogram.

Sew 5 onto 1 + 2 and 6 onto 3 + 4 and press again.

Sew 5 + 1 + 2 to 6 + 3 + 4. Press well. Make four of these units.

Starting where the star points intersect, stitch one side of a 4¾in background square to one star point and press. Stitch the other star point to the other side of the background square. Repeat for the other three background squares.

Join two quarters of the star together, starting where the star points intersect and sew one side of a background triangle to the star point. Press and then repeat for the other side of the

FINISHED SIZE

30cm (12in) square

MATERIALS

- 1½in strip across width of 3 different fabrics for the small parallelograms – cut the strip for the star point in half

- 2½in strip across width of 2 different fabrics for the large parallelograms or cut a template from the pattern sheet if you want to centre a design from your fabric – you need 4 large parallelograms of each fabric

- 4, 4¾in squares of background fabric

- 1, 7¼in square of background fabric cut into 4 through diagonals

- 33cm (13in) square of backing fabric for quilting

- 33cm (13in) square of Pellon

- 32cm x 34.5cm (12½in x 13½in) piece of fabric for cushion back

- 30cm (⅓yd) fabric for piping

- 1.5m (1⅝yd) of piping

- 35cm (14in) zipper

- Quilting thread and needle

- 30cm (12in) cushion insert

- General sewing supplies

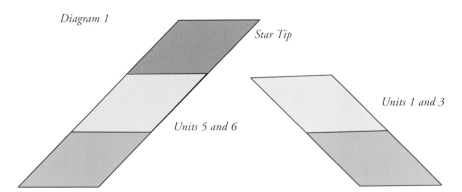

Diagram 1

Star Tip

Units 5 and 6

Units 1 and 3

Above: Cut strips for the Shell Cushion.

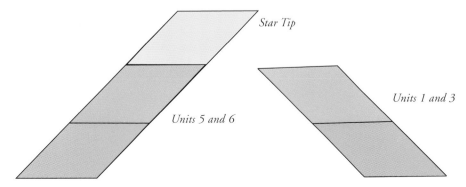

Star Tip

Units 5 and 6

Units 1 and 3

Right: Cut strips for the Pink Floral Cushion.

Block Assembly Diagram
For each of four units, sew 1 to 2 and 3 to 4.
Sew 5 onto 1+2 and 6 onto 3+4.
Sew 5+1+2 to 6+3+4.

background triangle. Do the same for the other two star quarters, then join the two halves together and insert the remaining two background triangles.

QUILTING

Layer the 13in squares of backing fabric, Pellon and the cushion top, right side up. Baste together through the three layers and quilt around the shapes. When your quilting is finished remove the basting and trim the cushion top to 12$\frac{1}{2}$in square.

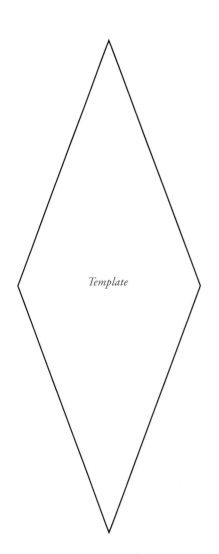

Template

Above: Use the template to centre a particular design in each shape or cut the shapes from the 2$\frac{1}{2}$in strip.

Below: Sew the 1$\frac{1}{2}$in strips together, fold in half and cut on a 45-degree angle at 1$\frac{1}{2}$in intervals.

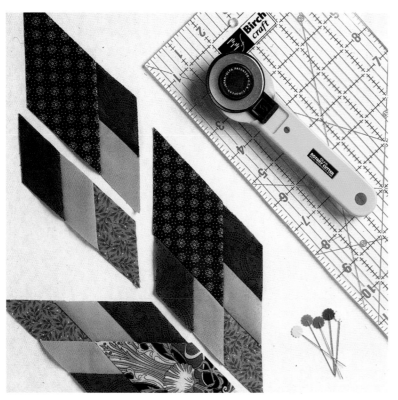

Above: Piece the strips and parallelograms together to form units. Then join units together in pairs.

Below: Stitch one side of the background square to one star point. Press and then stitch the other side of the background square to the other star point.

CUSHION CONSTRUCTION

Cut enough 1¼in strips of fabric on the bias for the piping. Join the strips together to form one continuous long strip. Fold the fabric over the piping and stitch along the strip to hold the piping in place using a zipper foot on your machine.

Starting in the middle of one side, raw edges together, stitch the piping to the edges of the cushion top.

Cut the cushion back fabric in half to form two, 12½in x 6¾in pieces. Press under ½in on one side of each rectangle for the zipper. Centre the zipper so the edges extend evenly past each end of the fabric and stitch in place using a zipper foot.

With the right sides together, start stitching the cushion back to the top, just past the zipper. Continue around the cushion until about 2in from the zipper. Open the zipper a few inches and finish stitching around the cushion. Open the zipper completely and turn the cushion right side out. Add the cushion insert and close the zipper. ✳

TIP

When assembling diamond shapes into a star design, here's a tip to ensure that the seam junctions fit snugly together without leaving little holes. Run a threaded needle through the tips of all the points in a circle and gently pull together to close the gap.

Pink Floral Cushion
Margaret cut the large parallelogram from the 2¹/₂ strip for this cushion.

Shell Cushion
Margaret used the template to centre a shell design in four of the large parallelograms for this design.

Basic Equipment

1	Paper Cutting Scissors	8	Needles	15	Rotary Cutter
2	Dressmaker's Scissors	9	HB Pencil	16	100% Cotton Thread
3	Embroidery Scissors	10	Silver Marking Pencil	17	Cotton/Polyester Thread
4	Tape Measure	11	Templates	18	Cutting Mat
5	Thimble	12	Glass-headed Pins	19	Safety Pins
6	Ruby Beholder	13	Plastic Ruler		
7	Adjustable Ruler	14	Pin Cushion		

BASIC EQUIPMENT

❖

We may have come a long way since quilts were first made in the 1880s, but the basic tools for patchwork such as needles, thread, pins and scissors remain the essentials.

NEEDLES

❖

For machine stitching you will need a supply of new sewing machine needles for light to medium-weight cottons.

A 'betweens' needle is considered the best for both hand piecing and quilting. 'Sharps' are used when a longer needle is required. A good general rule is to use as fine a needle as you can manage comfortably; size 8 is recommended for beginners. If you want to make smaller stitches as you progress, use a smaller needle. Size 12 is the smallest.

THREAD

❖

Traditionally, synthetic threads are used with synthetic fabrics and cotton with cotton fabrics. Polyester-cotton thread (polyester core wrapped in cotton) or 100 per cent cotton thread are best for cotton fabrics and are the easiest to use for all other fabrics. This thread does have a tendency to fray and tangle so avoid this by knotting the end before unrolling the thread, then cutting and threading the other end through the needle.

Select a colour that matches the darkest fabric you are sewing. If you are using different fabrics, select a neutral thread such as grey or ecru which will blend inconspicuously with all of them.

PINS

❖

Glass-headed pins are very sharp and good for piercing straight through the material when lining up a seam or a starting point.

There is a longer pin available which is excellent for pinning together layers on more bulky projects.

SCISSORS

❖

You will need three pairs of scissors for patchwork. Dressmaker's shears, preferably with a bent handle – these should be extremely sharp and used only for cutting fabric. Paper scissors – never cut paper with sewing shears, as this will dull the blades. Embroidery scissors for clipping threads and seam allowances – these should also be very sharp.

ROTARY CUTTER AND MAT

❖

A rotary cutter is an excellent tool for cutting strips, straightening fabric edges and cutting out a variety of geometric patchwork pieces. It also enables more accurate cutting of several layers of fabric at once.

Choose a cutter with a large blade, and keep spare blades handy. Always cut on a mat specially designed for a rotary cutter to keep the blade sharp. Fold the fabric in half on the mat with right sides facing and selvedges matching. The drafting triangle sits directly on the fold of the fabric, the rotary rule sits on the left edge of the triangle. The mat grips the fabric and helps the blade to cut straight. A 'self-healing' cutting mat is ideal.

RULERS

❖

A long, clear plastic ruler is a must to use with a rotary cutter. These rulers are well marked and sturdy and there is no danger of shaving off a piece of the ruler when cutting layers of fabric.

PENCILS

❖

A soft lead pencil is the traditional option for marking a design, but there is also a variety of marking pencils available. Probably the most useful is a water soluble pencil, as it gradually fades after a period of time.

Be careful, however, as the design is liable to disappear before the project can be finished.

TEMPLATES

❖

Templates can be homemade from graph paper, tracing paper and cardboard or template plastic. The edges of cardboard templates tend to wear after frequent cutting of patches, but plastic and metal templates, which are available in a great variety of shapes and sizes, are virtually indestructible. This is a great advantage, especially for a large project which requires cutting out several of each shape.

Window templates are useful if you are featuring or centring a motif or flower in a patch.

Templates for hand sewing, appliqué and quilting are cut to the exact shape without seam allowance. They mark the stitching line not the cutting line. For machine sewing, include 6mm (¼in) seam allowance around all edges.

THIMBLES

❖

A thimble is indispensable if you are quilting by hand. It is also good to use on the finger underneath the work to push the needle back through the fabric.

FRAMES AND HOOPS

❖

A frame or a hoop makes the quilting of large projects, such as bed-sized quilts, much easier. It is not essential to use one for smaller items, but you will get a better finish.

FABRICS

❖

Choosing the most suitable fabric for your patchwork project is important, especially for a beginner. Some fabrics are easier to work with than others. With experience, you will discover which fabric is a joy to use and which is an absolute headache. The most important rules to remember are to buy the best fabric you can afford. A firmly woven, lightweight, 100 per cent pure cotton is easier to use, lasts longer and gives crisp results.

Synthetics and mixtures can be difficult to iron and handle and may pucker along the seams but they are attractive, versatile and can be unusual or striking in appearance. They are often more readily available than 100 per cent cottons, but they are not all easier to use. Some tend to be slippery, floppy and soft.

As you gain experience, you may want to experiment with more exotic fabrics. Many of these will need special handling but to find out about these fabrics, you will have to test them yourself. Some satins and taffeta can be too fragile for patchwork. Synthetics also tend to be more difficult to quilt through as they are slightly spongy.

COLOURS AND PRINTS

❖

The successful combining of colours is often a matter of trial and error, not something that can be taught. The only way to find out if it will work is by trying it.

To achieve a good contrast, you need a mix of prints: small, medium, large, checks, stripes and plains. A mix of colours is also important. Contrast rather than coordinate. You will need a mixture of colour values – twenty per cent darks, forty per cent mediums and forty per cent lights is a good mix.

The value, or the lightness or darkness of a colour, is probably more important than the actual colour when you are making a quilt. To achieve successful results, try to use a range of values.

Many small-scale floral prints are available. Although a safe choice, they are sometimes so safe and well colour-coordinated that they give a rather dull and uninspired finished effect.

Experiment with prints of varying scale, stripes and border designs, geometric prints and checks. Some large-scale prints can introduce a delicate, lacy effect. Take particular care with stripes. If they are not cut and sewn perfectly straight, it will be very obvious.

Certain fabrics are evocative of different eras or styles. Create a country-style quilt by including fabrics which are bold and brightly coloured and include different-sized checks, stripes, ticking, stars and geometric prints.

A 1930s-style quilt can be created by including fabrics such as bright pastels, fresh florals, perky checks, stripes and white backgrounds.

FABRICS TO AVOID

❖

Stretch fabrics such as knits and some crepes should always be avoided. Very closely woven fabrics can also prove difficult, even for machine sewing. This applies to heavy fabrics such as canvas, and lightweight fabrics like some poplins.

Very open weave fabrics can cause difficulties with fraying and because of their transparency.

PREPARATION OF FABRICS

❖

Always wash your fabrics before use. This will pre-shrink them, remove excess dye and remove any sizing, so that the fabric is easier to handle. Machine wash your fabrics unless you have only a small quantity of fabric.

The volume of water used for washing seems to flush the dye and sizing out thoroughly. It is unusual to have a problem such as the dye running from one fabric to others, but if you are not sure of a fabric, always hand wash it separately.

If tumble drying, a short drying time is quite sufficient, unless the pieces are very large.

Don't over-dry fabrics, as they may become very creased. Remove while they are still slightly damp, then iron them.

When you are purchasing batting for your quilt, it is important to read the washing instructions before you make your choice. Some synthetic battings are often unsuitable for ordinary laundering. Always choose natural fibre battings such as wool, cotton or silk. A good mixture is 90 per cent cotton and 10 per cent polyester. This blend is suitable for both hand and machine quilting and it also washes very well.

Conversion Chart for Fabrics

In that cupboard full of treasured fabrics that every dedicated quilter owns, there are special favourites that are only 90cm wide, when you need 115cm or 150cm width for a special project. Our chart below will show you how to convert the fabric to the width you need.

WIDTH	90cm	115cm	150cm
MEASUREMENT	1.6m	1.3m	0.9m
	1.8m	1.5m	1.1m
	2.1m	1.6m	1.3m
	2.3m	1.9m	1.5m
	2.6m	2.1m	1.6m
	2.9m	2.3m	1.7m
	3.1m	2.5m	1.8m
	3.4m	2.6m	2.1m
	3.9m	2.9m	2.2m
	4.1m	3.1m	2.4m
	4.3m	3.3m	2.5m
	4.6m	3.5m	2.6m

If one of your favourite fabrics is 90cm wide and the size you require is 2.5m x 115cm, go down to the 2.5m in the 115cm column and directly across to the 90cm column. You will need 3.1m of the 90cm fabric for the same project. Remember to allow a little more for napped fabric.

Basic Instructions

Patchwork quilts can be made in many different ways. Here we give you the basic techniques required to successfully complete a quilt.

DESIGN AND DRAFTING

To adapt a design or border, or see how the quilt will look and fit together, you will need to make a sketch on graph paper.

Graph paper is used for two things – to make small sketches of quilt designs (graph plan) and to make full size drawings of shapes for templates or as guides for rotary cutting.

You can play with different colourings with a graph plan and use it as a reference map as you construct your quilt. This helps to see the relative proportions of the border and quilt and to judge the effect. A sketch also lets you preview your quilt and make improvements before you start cutting and sewing.

A quilt sketch is a drawing of the quilt in miniature. You will need to assign a scale in order to calculate the finished size of the quilt and to draft templates. Keep the scale easy so that cutting dimensions will match standard markings on your rotary cutting ruler.

DRAFTING TEMPLATES

Graph paper marked in ¼in is one of the easiest to use to make full size drawings of template shapes. You can draw a full size block or portion of a border onto graph paper and identify each shape to be cut by lightly colouring it in, then add a consistent ¼in seam allowance around each one. Trace the completed shapes onto template material or use the measurements as cutting guides for template-free rotary cutting.

Template plastic with a ¼in grid is also available, so that shapes can be drawn directly onto it and an accurate seam allowance should be added. If the templates are to be used for machine sewing, add a ¼in seam allowance all around. If the template is being used for hand sewing, add a ¼in seam allowance when cutting out the fabric. Straight grain arrows should be marked onto templates.

Note: The outside edges of a block or quilt must always be on the straight grain, or the quilt will not lie flat. Mark your graphed blocks and borders accordingly.

Glueing a piece of sandpaper to the back of a paper or plastic template, with the gritty side facing down, is a great way of cutting accurate shapes from fabric.

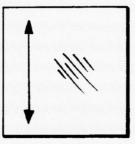

Standard Template

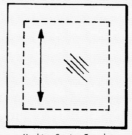

Machine Sewing Template

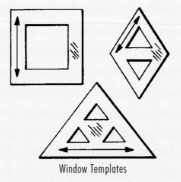

Window Templates

The sandpaper adds weight and sturdiness and the rough surface grips the fabric for more accurate cutting.

Note: Do not cut your sandpaper with fabric scissors.

CUTTING

Trim the selvedge from the fabric before you begin. If you are using one fabric for both borders and block pieces, cut the borders first, then the block pieces from what is left over.

Position templates on fabric so that the arrows match the straight grain. With a sharp pencil (an erasable pencil or a white for dark fabrics, or lead pencil for light fabrics), trace around the template on the fabric. Allow a further ¼in all around the drawn shape for seam allowance before cutting out. Templates for machine sewing include a seam allowance, but these pieces must be precisely cut as there is no drawn line to guide your sewing. Multiple layers can be cut at the one time by folding and pressing the fabric into layers before placing the template. Make sure that each piece is cut on the straight grain.

ROTARY OR TEMPLATE-FREE CUTTING

It is important to use the rotary cutter accurately and efficiently to ensure straight pieces. Straighten the fabric by folding it in layers, selvedge to selvedge, to fit on the cutting mat. Lay a triangle along the folded edge of the fabric and push it against the right side of the ruler until it is just at the edge.

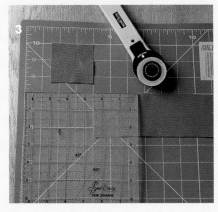

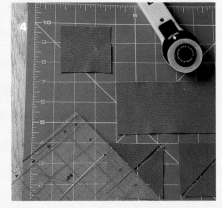

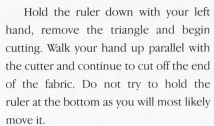

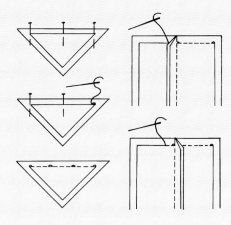

Hold the ruler down with your left hand, remove the triangle and begin cutting. Walk your hand up parallel with the cutter and continue to cut off the end of the fabric. Do not try to hold the ruler at the bottom as you will most likely move it.

Once you have straightened the fabric, use the cutter and ruler to cut strips of fabric to the width you require.

Squares, rectangles and triangles are all cut from strips. Remember when cutting squares and rectangles to add ½in to the desired finished measurement. For a 2in finished square cut a 2½in square. For a 2in x 4in finished rectangle, cut 2½in x 4½in.

Half square triangles are half a square with the short sides on the straight grain and the long side on the bias. To cut these triangles, cut a square in half diagonally. Cut the square ⅞in larger than the finished short side of the triangle to allow for seam allowances.

Quarter square triangles are used along the outside edge of a quilt

and some blocks are quarter square triangles. These triangles have their short sides on the bias and the long side on the straight grain. These triangles are cut from squares. Each square is cut into four on the diagonal and each is 1¼in larger than the finished long side of the triangle.

PIECING METHODS

Hand Piecing

Pieces for hand piecing require precisely marked seamlines; marked cutting lines are optional.

Place the template face down on the wrong side of the fabric and draw around it accurately with a sharp pencil. Leave space between patches for a ¼in seam allowance when cutting.

After marking the patches, cut outward from the seamline ¼in, measuring the distance by eye. Join the

pieces right sides together, so the marked seamline on the wrong side of the fabric is visible on both sides of the patchwork when sewing. Sew the seam through the pencilled lines with a short running stitch and occasional Backstitch, using a single thread.

Begin and end each seam at the seamline (not at the edge of fabric) with two or three Backstitches to secure the seam and sew from point to point, not edge to edge.

When joining the blocks and the rows together, do not sew the seam allowance down. Sew up to the dot marking the corner, then begin on the next side by taking a couple of extra small Backstitches and continue sewing along the line. This leaves your options open as to which way to press the seam allowance when the block is completed.

English Paper Piecing Method

This hand piecing technique involves basting fabric over a thin cardboard or paper template. The shapes are stitched together to form blocks and ultimately to form a quilt.

Although time-consuming, this method results in precise, sharp seams and a professionally finished appearance for your project. It also has the advantage of being able to be picked up, put down and carried around so you can work on your project in those spare moments.

Make a master template shape from firm plastic. On gift board, trace the required quantity of each shape. On the wrong side of the selected fabric, trace the required amount of each shape. Cut these out with a generous ¼in seam allowance.

Place the cardboard template in the centre of the wrong side of the fabric shape. Working one side at a time, fold over the seam allowance onto the template. Baste into place through the template, making sure the corners of the fabric are neatly folded in. For easy removal of the basting, start with a knot and finish with a simple double stitch.

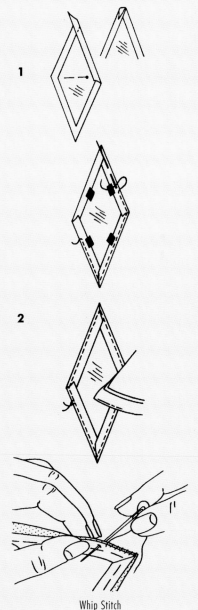

1

2

Whip Stitch

To join the patches together, place them right sides facing and match corners. With a matching thread, or a mid-grey thread which blends with most colours, join the edges from corner to corner using a tiny Whipstitch and double stitch the corners. The stitch should be fairly small and not visible from the right side of the fabric.

Make each block separately by sewing the smallest pieces together first to form units. Join smaller units to form larger ones until the block is complete.

Press, then join the blocks together to form rows and the rows together to form the sampler or quilt top.

The cardboard templates can be removed when all the pieces are joined together. Turn the quilt over, press well with a warm iron and allow to cool. Carefully remove the basting stitches and lift out each piece of cardboard separately.

Machine Piecing

Accurate cutting is very important especially in machine piecing. Include seam allowances in the template and mark the cutting line on the back of the fabric.

Use white or neutral thread as light in colour as the lightest colour in the project. Use a dark neutral thread for piecing dark solids.

When machine sewing patches, align cut edges with the edge of the presser foot if it is ¼in wide. If not, place masking tape on the throat plate of the machine ¼in away from the needle to guide you in making ¼in seams. Sew along to the cut edge unless you are inserting a patch into an angle. Short seams need not be pinned unless matching is involved. Keep pins away from the seamline. Sewing over pins is not good for sewing machine needles.

Use chain-piecing whenever it is possible in order to save valuable time and thread. Sew one seam, however do

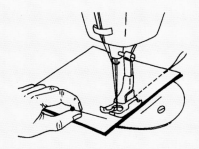

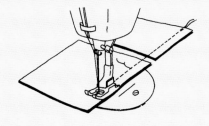

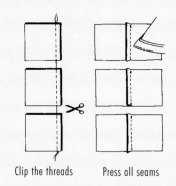

Clip the threads   Press all seams

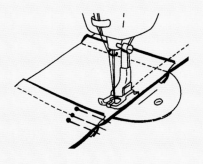

not lift the presser foot. Do not take the piece out of the sewing machine and do not cut the thread.

Instead, you should set up the next piece to be sewn and continue stitching. There will be small twists of thread between the two pieces. Sew all the seams you can at one time, then remove the 'chain'. Clip all of the threads, then press the seams.

When joining rows, make sure matching seam allowances are pressed in opposite directions to reduce bulk and make matching easier. Pin pieces together directly through stitching and to the right or left of the seam, removing the pins as you sew.

JOINING BLOCKS

❖

Blocks joined edge to edge

Join the blocks to form strips the width of the quilt. Pin each seam very carefully, inserting a pin wherever seams meet, at right angles to the seam using a ¼in seam allowance. Join all blocks in the second row, continuing until all rows are completed. Press all seam allowances in the odd-numbered rows in one direction and all seam allowances in even-numbered rows in the opposite direction. When all rows are completed, pin two rows together so that seamlines match perfectly. Join rows in groups of two, then four, and so on until the top is completed. Press all allowances in one direction, either up or down.

Blocks joined with vertical and horizontal sashing

Join the blocks into strips with a vertical sash between each pair of blocks. Sew a horizontal piece of sashing to each strip, then join the strips to form the quilt top.

PRESSING

❖

Press the seam allowances to one side, usually towards the darker fabric. Press quilt blocks flat and square with no puckers. To correct any problems in blocks, sashes or borders, remove a few stitches to ease puckers and re-sew.

APPLIQUE

❖

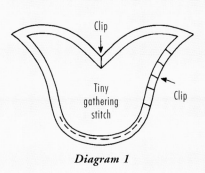

Diagram 1

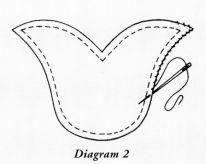

Diagram 2

Appliqué is not a difficult technique but basic rules do apply. Curved shapes should be smooth with no points, points should be a definite point, and there should be no puckers. Begin by marking around the template onto the right side of the fabric. Cut out the shape with a ¼in seam allowance. Turn the seam allowance under and baste. When there is a sharp curve sew a tiny running stitch just to the outside of the marked line. Gather slightly so that the curve sits well (see Diagram 1). Where there is a sharp point, mitre the corner as you are basting, and cut away any excess fabric. Be careful not to cut away too much. Pin the pieces to the background fabric making sure they are centred.

Cut a 15¾in length of thread and make a small knot. Make sure the knot sits underneath the piece being appliquéd, then bring the thread from the back through the background fabric and catch a couple of threads on the appliqué piece. When you begin to appliqué, make sure the needle enters the background fabric directly opposite

where it came out on the top piece and slightly under the piece being appliquéd (see Diagram 2). When you have completed stitching, finish off on the back with a couple of small Backstitches.

ADDING MITRED BORDERS

❖

Centre a border strip each side of the quilt top to extend equally at each end. Pin, baste, and sew strips in ¼in seams, beginning and ending at the seamline, not the outer edge of the fabric. At one corner, on the wrong side, smooth one border over the adjacent one and draw a diagonal line from the inner seamline to the point where the outer edges of the two borders cross. Reverse the two borders (the bottom one is now on top), draw a diagonal line from the inner seamline to the point where the outer edges cross. Match the two pencil lines (fabrics right sides together), and sew through them. Cut away the excess, and press the allowances open. Repeat at the other corners of the quilt.

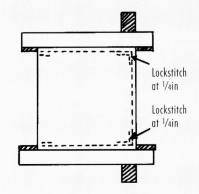

Lockstitch at ¼in

Lockstitch at ¼in

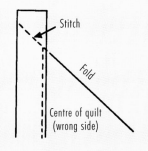

Stitch

Fold

Centre of quilt (wrong side)

BATTING

❖

Batting is the padding that plumps up the quilt. It goes between the quilt top and the backing. There is a variety of battings on the market, ranging from natural fibres such as cotton and wool to synthetics. Most battings are available in different weights, but a thin, lightweight one is ideal for hand quilting, as it is much easier to produce small, even stitches. A thin batting also gives a more authentic appearance to traditional quilt designs. Thicker battings are useful if you want extra warmth and they can be tied rather than quilted.

BACKING

❖

Make the quilt backing about 2in larger each side than the quilt top. The two or three lengths that need to be sewn must be seamed together. Remove the selvedges to avoid puckers and press the seam allowances open or to one side. Place the backing, wrong side up, on a flat surface. Spread quilt batting over the backing, making sure that both stay smooth and even. Place the quilt top,

right side up, on top of the batting. Pin layers as necessary to secure them while basting. Beginning in the centre, baste in an 'X'. Working outwards, baste rows 4in and 6in apart. Baste all around the edges.

MARKING FOR QUILTING

❖

Place a quilting pattern under the quilt top. Lightly mark the design on the top, using a hard lead pencil. Mark dark-coloured fabrics with a chalk pencil. Always test water-soluble pens for removability before marking the quilt. Some quilting may be done without marking the top. Outline quilting ¼in from seam around patches or quilting in the ditch (right next to the seam on the side without the seam allowances) can be done by 'marking' the quilting line by eye. Other straight lines may also be marked as you quilt by using a piece of masking tape that is pulled away after a line is quilted along the edge.

QUILTING

❖

Quilting is done in a short running stitch with a single strand of thread that goes through all three layers. Use a short needle (8 or 9 betweens) with about 18in thread. Make a small knot in the thread and take a first long stitch, about 1in, through the top and batting only, coming up where the quilting will begin. Tug on the thread to pull the knotted end between the layers. Take straight, even stitches that are the same size on the top and bottom of the quilt. For tiny stitches, push the needle with a thimble on your middle finger. Guide the fabric in front of the needle with the thumb of your hand

above the quilt and with the thumb and index finger of your other hand below the quilt. To end a line of quilting, take a tiny Back Stitch, make another small knot and pull between the layers. Make another 1in long stitch through the top and batting only and clip the thread at the surface of the quilt. Carefully pull out the basting threads when the quilting is finished.

BINDING

❖

Trim the edges of the quilt. One of the most popular methods of binding is to cut the binding fabric into seven 3in strips, selvedge to selvedge. Join these to make one long strip and press in half along the length, wrong sides together. Sew to the quilt top, starting at the centre bottom, ½in from the raw edges. To mitre the binding, stop ½in from the corner, Backstitch and take out of the machine.

Fold the binding up making a 45 degree angle with the binding strip.

Fold down, level with the edge and sew to the next corner. Repeat and over-lap the ends of the binding, Slip Stitch in place to the back of the quilt. A nice finishing touch is to embroider your name, city, and date on the back of the quilt.

CARE OF QUILTS

❖

After spending many hours making a quilt you will want to look after it in the best possible way. Remember, it may well become a future heirloom.

While you obviously want to use and enjoy your quilt, you also want to minimise the amount of wear and tear it receives. Get into the habit of folding back the quilt at night so it lies across the foot of the bed only. Or remove it entirely. In this age of electric blankets and heated waterbeds, a quilt is often decorative rather than functional. If you do need the quilt for warmth at night, place a sheet underneath it.

Turn it back over the top edge of the quilt with at least a metre turn back. This will greatly reduce soiling.

Quilts made from suitable fabrics can be washed successfully, but if you care for your quilt properly, you will reduce the need for frequent washing.

Sunlight weakens the fabric fibres and also fades the colours. If the bed receives direct sunlight it is wise to fold back the quilt or draw the curtains.

STORAGE

❖

Store your quilt by rolling or folding it and wrapping it in an old cotton pillowcase or sheet.

If it is folded, it should be refolded occasionally along different fold lines to avoid permanent creasing.

Never store in a plastic bag as air circulation is essential.

Do not place an unwrapped quilt directly on a wooden shelf as chemicals in the timber can stain the fabric.

WASHING

❖

If possible, hand wash the quilt in a large container such as the bath. Use warm, not hot water and dissolve the detergent before adding the quilt. Soak for 5 to 10 minutes then squeeze gently by hand; do not twist or wring. Rinse thoroughly in lukewarm water. If you want to use fabric conditioner make sure it is stirred into

the rinse water and not poured directly onto the quilt.

If you have a washing machine large enough to take the quilt without having to cram it in, spin the quilt to remove excess water, as the excess weight of water can strain the stitching. Use a low speed spin if you have the option.

Dry the quilt outdoors away from direct sunlight. Spread it flat on a clean sheet, or drape it over a patio table. If using the clothesline, spread the quilt over several parallel lines rather than

hanging the entire weight of the quilt from one line.

The quilt can be machine washed if you don't have a large enough container. However, do not try to wash a large quilt in a small machine as it cannot be cleaned effectively and the lack of space can damage the quilt. Once the quilt is dry, place it in a tumble dryer on a cool cycle to fluff up the batting.

If the quilt needs to be ironed, place it right side down on a thick towel and steam press gently on the wrong side. ❀

Continuous Bias Binding

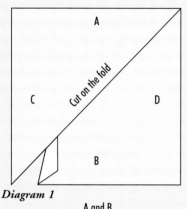

Diagram 1

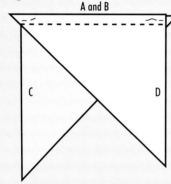

Diagram 2

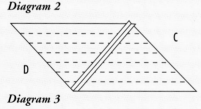

Diagram 3

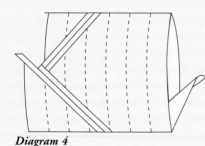

Diagram 4

Diagram 5

Continuous bias binding is a useful method of cutting bias strips for binding a quilt or for appliqué stems.

It is made from a square of fabric on the straight grain, cut in half diagonally. The length and width of the bias needed determines the size of the square required. The square size should be evenly divisible by the required width of the binding. Refer the step by step Continuous Bias diagrams.

With right sides together, pin and sew with a short machine stitch along the two short sides of the cut triangles with a ¼in seam. Press seam open. This creates a parallelogram. Using a large ruler or dressmaker's square, mark the finished cut width on the wrong side of the fabric on the bias grain. Connect marks with a straight line. With right sides together and dropping down one bias width, match pencil markings and pin. There can

sometimes be a small amount of fabric left when marking the cutting lines. Ignore this and continue to make the binding, then cut the small amount off when the bias is complete. Sew the unit together to form a tube, as shown in the diagrams. Begin cutting on the marked lines to form one long strip. This method allows an economical use of fabric and a true bias is achieved.

BIAS STRIP CALCULATIONS

To estimate the size of the square required for a given length of bias:

Multiply the length of the strip by the cut width of the strip to find the area. This will give you the size of the square needed to yield the required length.

To find the size, using a calculator, press the square root button (square root symbol) and round the number up.

For example, if your quilt requires approximately 300in of 2½in-wide binding, $300 \times 2\frac{1}{2} = 750$. The square root of 750 is 27.4, so you will need a 28in square.

To estimate the length of bias that can be cut from a square:

Multiply the width of the square by the length of the square to find the area.

Divide the area of the square by the width of the binding strip to find the length of the strip that can be cut.

For example, if you have a 20in square to cut 2½in-wide binding, 2½in will divide into the square eight times.

Multiply 8 x 20in (one side of the square) to find this method will yield approximately 160in of binding.   ✳

Continuous Bias Diagrams

1. Cut a square in half on the diagonal.
2. With right sides together, stitch A to B with a ¼in seam allowance. Overlap points of A and B.
3. Press the seam open and mark lines the width of the required strip along the bias edge.
4. With right sides together and dropping down one bias width, match pencil markings, pin and sew to form a tube.
5. Cut on the marked lines to form one long strip.

Index

Published by
Craftworld Books
A division of Express Publications Pty Ltd, ACN 057 807 904
Under licence from EP Investments Pty Ltd, ACN 003 109 055 (1995)

2 Stanley Street
Silverwater NSW 2128
Australia

First published by Craftworld Books 2000

Publisher Sue Aiken
Photographic Director Robyn Wilson
Editor Sue Aiken
Production Editor Annie Davis
Designer Rachel Kirkland
Technical Consultant Becky Peters

Photographers Tim Connolly, Mark Heriot
Stylists Robyn Wilson, Sue Aiken

National Library of Australia Cataloguing-in-Publication data

Bright & Beautiful Quilts

Includes index
ISBN 187562516X

1. Quilting

Printed by KHL Printing Co, Singapore

Australian distribution to supermarkets and newsagents by Network Distribution Company, 54 Park Street, Sydney NSW 2000 Ph (02) 9282 8777.
Australian book shop distribution by Gary Allen Book Distribution, 9 Cooper Street, Smithfield NSW 2164 Ph (02) 9725 2933
Overseas Distribution Enquiries Godfrey Vella Ph 61 (2) 9748 0599, Locked Bag 111, Silverwater NSW 1811 Australia
email: gvella@expresspublications.com.au website: www.expresspublications.com.au